Implementing Real Change in Human Resources Management

658.3 St82
Strategies and alternatives
for transforming human

Strategies and Alternatives for Transforming Human Resources Management

Panel Members

Patricia W. Ingraham, *Panel Chair*
Thomas P. Carney
James E. Colvard
Elizabeth L. Hollander
Constance J. Horner
Madelyn P. Jennings
Michael R. Losey
Elsa A. Porter
Gordon M. Sherman
John N. Sturdivant

The views expressed in this document are those of the contributors alone. They do not necessarily reflect the views of the Academy as an institution.

National Academy of Public Administration
1120 G Street, NW
8th Floor
Washington, DC 20005

First published 1995
Second printing 1996

Printed in the United States of America

The paper used in this publication meets the minimum requirements of American National Standard for Information Sciences – Permanence of Paper for Printed Library Materials, ANSI Z39.48-1984.

ISBN 0-9646874-3-7(pbk)
Strategies & Alternatives For Transforming Human Resources Management

Officers of the Academy

Peter Szanton, *Chair of the Board*
C. William Fischer, *Vice Chair*
R. Scott Fosler, *President*
Feather O' Connor Houstoun, *Secretary*
Howard Messner, *Treasurer*

Project Staff

Frank P. Cipolla, *Project Director*
Curt L. Dierdorff, *Assistant Project Director*
Rebecca J. Wallace, *Senior Research Associate*
Julia K. Oster, *Programs Assistant*
Julie A. Everitt, *Research Assistant*
Jennifer L. Lipnick, *Research Assistant*
Jill M. Grecco, *Research Assistant*

PREFACE

This report provides sponsoring agencies with alternatives and strategies for transforming human resources management within their organizations. Agencies can implement many of the suggested actions within existing authorities. Some of the actions will require additional statutory authorities and/or government-wide policy changes. Specific legislative proposals are not included. Rather, the report identifies areas where legislation is necessary to improve government's human resources management and better accomplish mission results.

The specific policy or legislative changes required to enable agencies to fully transform human resources management will be addressed in more detail in the final report which will integrate the conclusions and recommendations of all three components of the National Academy of Public Administration (NAPA) Human Resources Management (HRM) Project: Classification Broad-Banding; HRM Redefinition; and the Educational-Informational Programs on Labor-Management Partnerships, Alternative Dispute Resolution, and Downsizing.

TABLE OF CONTENTS

PREFACE	v
LIST OF TABLES AND FIGURES	ix
GLOSSARY	xi
EXECUTIVE SUMMARY	xiii

CHAPTER 1
Introduction ... 1

CHAPTER 2
Aligning HRM System With Organizational Results ... 5

CHAPTER 3
HRM Roles, Systems and Accountability ... 9

CHAPTER 4
Structuring the Organization to Provide HRM Services ... 17

CHAPTER 5
Measurement ... 29

CHAPTER 6
Achieving More Effective Human Resources Management: A Strategy ... 35

APPENDIXES
Appendix A - Literature Review Summary ... 43
Appendix B - Focus Group Results ... 79
Appendix C - Factors Unique to Small Federal Agencies Report ... 103
Appendix D - Clusters of Functions ... 113

LIST OF TABLES AND FIGURES

TABLES

TABLE 1 - Expected Outcomes from an HRM System	8
TABLE 2 - Distribution of HRM Accountability Between HR and Line Managers	15
TABLE 3 - Criteria to Decide Where Human Resources Services Should Be Provided	19
TABLE 4 - A Proposed Service Delivery Model for HR Activities	20
TABLE 5 - Advantages and Disadvantages to a Shared Services Delivery Approach	23
TABLE 6 - HR Training Needs for Line Managers	37
TABLE 7 - A Supervisory and Leadership Skills Training Model	38
TABLE 8 - Skills and Competencies Needed by HR Staffs	39

FIGURES

FIGURE 1 - Drivers of HR's Involvement as a Strategic Partner	9
FIGURE 2 - Barriers to Federal Line Managers Control of HRM	11
FIGURE 3 - Conditions for Establishing HRM Accountability	14
FIGURE 4 - Factors Affecting the Choice of HR Service Delivery Models	17
FIGURE 5 - Proposed "Clusters" of HR Functions	18
FIGURE 6 - What to Measure?	30
FIGURE 7 - Value-Added Model for HRM	36
FIGURE 8 - A Model for HR Staff Development	40

GLOSSARY

Automated Data Processing	**ADP**
American Telephone and Telegraph	**AT&T**
Chief Executive Officer	**CEO**
Commission on Reform and Efficiency	**CORE**
Civilian Personnel Management Service	**CPMS**
Department of Defense	**DoD**
Equal Employment Opportunity	**EEO**
Equal Employment Opportunity Commission	**EEOC**
Fair Labor Standards Act	**FLSA**
U.S. General Accounting Office	**GAO**
Government Performance and Results Act	**GPRA**
Department of Health and Human Services	**HHS**
Hewlett-Packard	**HP**
Human Resource(s)	**HR**
Human Resource(s) Management	**HRM**
Management Information Systems	**MIS**
U.S. Merit Systems Protection Board	**MSPB**
National Academy of Public Administration	**NAPA**
National Performance Review	**NPR**
Office of Management and Budget	**OMB**
Office of Personnel Management	**OPM**
Occupational Safety and Health Administration	**OSHA**
Total Quality Management	**TQM**

EXECUTIVE SUMMARY

Change is an inevitable part of today's workplace. To stay competitive or to meet the demands of the public they serve, organizations, private and public, must innovate to become more effective and efficient. If Drucker is correct and "knowledge is becoming our most important product," then organizations must find better ways to recruit, develop, lead and nurture the human components of the organization who are the source of organizational knowledge and performance. This is the challenge for human resources management (HRM) today.

ALIGNING HRM SYSTEM WITH ORGANIZATIONAL RESULTS

Ultimately, the results HRM achieves must be synonymous with organizational success. Human Resources (HR) practices and activities must be relevant to the organizational challenges line managers face. HRM work must be connected to the organization's mission requirements.

The National Academy of Public Administration (NAPA) found considerable evidence that the private sector has moved forward aggressively to link human resources to companies' strategic goals. Despite the Government Performance and Results Act (GPRA), which requires federal agencies to describe how they will use human resources to meet goals established in their 5-year strategic plans, there is limited evidence that agencies are effectively linking the human component to organizational strategy.

Specific actions to improve the alignment of HRM with agency goals and strategies are:

- Use GPRA strategic plans and NPR performance agreements with the president as vehicles to link tailored approaches to HRM with improved mission results.

- Actively involve HR staffs in developing GPRA strategic plans and NPR performance agreements which identify specific HR initiatives designed to enhance achievement of mission results.

- Congress should permit agencies to waive statutory requirements as they develop tailored approaches to HRM if such waivers would advance agency program results, within the context of basic principles such as equal employment

The National Academy of Public Administration (NAPA) found considerable evidence that the private sector has moved forward aggressively to link human resources to companies' strategic goals.

Executive Summary

When HR serves as a strategic partner, it is part of the leadership team when decisions that affect the future of the organization are discussed and debated.

opportunity (EEO), merit hiring and promotion, and health and safety programs. Oversight of agency waivers should be provided by means of normal Office of Management and Budget (OMB) and congressional program reviews.

- The Office of Personnel Management (OPM) should establish, or facilitate creation of, a clearinghouse of best practices that agencies can use to design approaches to more closely align HRM with agency strategy and program goals.

HRM ROLES, SYSTEMS AND ACCOUNTABILITY

To align HR programs and processes with mission goals and results, HR managers must serve as a strategic partner with management. Literature reviewed and interviews with innovative practice firms showed that the HR strategic role is emerging as the primary focus of leading-edge HR staffs. When HR serves as a strategic partner, it is part of the leadership team when decisions that affect the future of the organization are discussed and debated. HR's specific contribution to this process is to ensure that people issues associated with achieving future organizational goals are understood and considered. To perform at this level in the organization, HR professionals will need to develop knowledge of mission requirements as well as HR specialties.

Private sector firms that NAPA visited accept the principle that line managers are responsible and accountable for HRM. Although that principle appears to be generally accepted in the federal sector as well, there are barriers which must be overcome to move from theory to practice: HR system complexity; unclear expectations regarding mission results; a focus on procedures rather than results; inadequate information technology deployment; systemic and statutory limitations to tailoring HR policy to mission needs; insufficient training for managers on HR principles and techniques; a culture that discourages risk taking; and insufficient leadership continuity at the top of federal organizations.

In addition to overcoming these barriers, agencies must ensure that the organizational environment fosters concern for accountability for positive HRM practices. To help create such an environment, agencies can:

- Establish clear HRM goals tied to desired mission results;
- Focus on values rather than detailed rules;
- Provide adequate training and information so that it is clear what managers are accountable for;
- Demonstrate top line management leadership by example;
- Reward outstanding support for HRM values and enforce consequences for willful violations of values in a clear and forthright manner; and
- Develop measurement systems to determine whether HRM values are taking hold in the organization.

Just as line managers must be held accountable for HRM results, HR staff accountability must shift to focus on achieving business or mission results.

Efforts underway to reduce the size and scope of government will result in changes to agencies' relationships with employees similar to what is already occurring in the private sector. Federal employees will need to become more accountable for their performance and responsible for their career development, and they must perform some of the activities traditionally handled by HR offices.

Agencies can improve HRM by:

- Taking action to establish and reinforce HR's role as a strategic partner through involvement in discussion, formulation, and deployment of mission strategies and goals;
- Making an investment to develop HR staff competence to function in all role dimensions discussed in this report;
- Establishing and enforcing line managers' leadership of, and accountability for, HRM;
- Creating an environment that mitigates the barriers to accountability by simplifying and decentralizing the HR system, increasing the use of information technology, improving HRM focus on results, providing management training, creating a culture that tolerates risk, and promoting management continuity; and
- Initiating action to build greater employee self-reliance for their employability, for ensuring the accuracy of their personnel data, and administering their benefits package.

STRUCTURING THE ORGANIZATION TO PROVIDE HRM SERVICES

The federal government typically organizes HR service delivery models along functional specialization lines. To provide more integrated programs and services, HR needs to move away from these narrow, technical perspectives of its services. Agency leaders should do whatever they can to reengineer their HR work. HR reengineering activities need to be guided by three key questions:

- **Does the work need to be done?**
  If the customer does not value an HR activity and it is not dictated by legal or regulatory requirements, it should be eliminated.
- **Can the work be outsourced to achieve cost savings or improve service?**
  Agencies need to develop criteria for deciding what HR activities can be outsourced. NAPA's interviews revealed a number of HR activities that are being outsourced and others that federal employees and managers consider candidates for outsourcing.
- **If kept in-house, how can the work be done better?**
  Several factors affect the choice of HR service delivery models: organizational culture; organizational size; mission of the department or agency; geographic dispersion of the workforce; resource availability; the extent to which processes are automated; and client expectations.

For services provided in-house, NAPA found a variety of service delivery approaches that can best be described along a continuum from totally centralized to totally decentralized. Depending on the service provided, organizations offer them at a number of places along the continuum.

Executive Summary

The federal government typically organizes HR service delivery models along functional specialization lines. To provide more integrated programs and services, HR needs to move away from these narrow, technical perspectives of its services.

Executive Summary

Organizations need access to HR resources that can provide advice and assistance to resolve business-specific issues.

Routine Processing Activities

Transaction-based activities, which are generally administrative and routine in nature, are increasingly being automated and moved to a shared-services delivery model. Service centers perform such common activities as benefits administration, compensation and pay processing, training, and records management. They process the paperwork and provide consulting advice related to administrative transactions. These operations are supported by sophisticated information technology, often using telephone response systems (available 24 hours a day) and networks and telecommunications reaching all employees. Some organizations have chosen to have regional service centers. Others have chosen to have one center that services the entire country.

The literature review and NAPA's interviews in the public and private sector identified advantages and disadvantages to the shared services delivery approach. Advantages include: decreased cost; increased efficiency; increased productivity; elimination of duplicative and overlapping work; and greater flexibility to meet customer needs. Disadvantages are: feelings of depersonalized service; potential emergence of shadow staffs; costs to set up shared service centers and establish the needed technology base; and organizational resistance to losing on-site support.

Advisory and Consultative Activities

Organizations need access to HR resources that can provide advice and assistance to resolve business-specific issues. These HR professionals serve as advisors and consultants to managers to help implement business strategies and goals. They bring to the table organizational change strategies that will help a business unit achieve desired results. They also have the expert HR knowledge to access the resources needed to develop new programs and processes.

One model for delivering these types of HR services is to align HR advisory and consultative resources directly with the organizational units. By maintaining on-site personnel professionals who can consult with managers on organization-specific issues, HR can be more involved in correlating personnel knowledge and practice with organization challenges. These HR generalists generally have either a dotted-line or direct reporting relationship to the corporate HR office. The main advantage to this alignment of HR resources is that it helps the HR staff stay in touch with the needs of the organization and create solutions that are organization relevant and avoids "creating solutions looking for a strategy." A disadvantage is the amount of resources required to provide these services to all organizational units.

Another model for providing these non-routine, and non-administrative, organization consultant-type HR activities is the shared services environment. Individuals with extensive knowledge and expertise in organizational design and development, communication and other HR specialties are combined to work for Centers of Excellence rather than individual units. The organizational units use these shared resources to solve problems. Centers of Excellence have advantages and disadvantages similar to those noted for service centers. An additional difficulty may be the inability of a single HR entity to deal with multiple organizational missions and emphases embodied in the Center's customers. HR staff may find it difficult to understand a variety of missions and be flexible to tailor their advice to a variety of customers who may have different organizational priorities and values.

HR as a Strategic Partner

A shared service delivery model is not the optimum approach for the strategic partner activities. HR strategic partners ideally should be on-site, aligned with the top management team at the corporate and organization unit level and dedicated to those organizational units. Costs of providing a strategic partner for each organization are a disadvantage to this approach.

The implications for agencies as they develop HR service delivery models are:
- HR's customers should help HR determine which HR practices and activities should be performed or discarded.
- Practices and activities that are not valued by HR's customers should be eliminated if not required by laws or regulations.
- Key HR processes should be reengineered and automated.
- Even if an organization does not have the time/resources to reengineer its HR function, it should realign HR activities to provide more coherent planning and service delivery. This can be done by combining HR's many specialty areas into a few functional clusters along the lines suggested in this chapter. The use of HR generalists for service delivery is a promising trend. This trend will contribute to simpler and more effective support to line managers and employees.
- Departments and agencies should develop criteria for how work should be performed — contracted out, franchised, or done internally — and then use the criteria to complete a rigorous review to determine the best service delivery method.
- For routine activities to be performed in-house, departments and agencies should consider shared services to achieve more efficient service delivery. Small agencies, in particular, should consider using shared services to better utilize limited resources.
- Strategic HR resources should be provided at the corporate (departmental) and business unit (bureau) levels if at all possible.

MEASUREMENT

Measurement is important to any operation and is key to reinventing human resources. While some efforts have been made to measure human resources efforts to link HR to mission accomplishment need attention. Fitz-enz identifies the following causes of resistance to measurement: habit, fear that results will be used for punitive purposes, disagreement over what to measure, and lack of knowledge that measurement can be used to help HR and the organization be more successful.

First and foremost, HR should focus on effectiveness measures—how does HRM help the organization achieve its mission results? Efficiency should also be measured. NAPA found that some of the successful private firms visited dealt with effectiveness first, and then turned their attention to driving down costs and being more efficient. Efficiency needs to be measured because controlling costs is an important consideration in managing the federal workforce. Trend data measure workforce demographics and enable

Executive Summary

First and foremost, HR should focus on effectiveness measures — how does HRM help the organization achieve its mission results?

Executive Summary

the organization to forecast events and plan actions needed to avoid problems and tailor solutions to future mission priorities.

The following actions will enhance agencies' abilities to use measurement as a tool to improve HR's ability to contribute to organizational mission, people and efficiency goals:

- Establish reporting and evaluation processes to ensure that HRM measurement captures information that is most important to agency mission results. Involve line managers in the process. The scope of this activity should include considering the human component of mission results included in GPRA strategic plans.
- Measure employee satisfaction on a regular basis. This information should be used to hold managers and HR staff accountable for effective HRM.
- Conduct regular surveys and structured interviews to assess satisfaction with HR services. This information is a key accountability tool to assess HR performance effectiveness, and to identify needed improvement initiatives.
- Train HR staffs in data analysis and statistical techniques so that they can evaluate program results and trends as a basis for improving HR operations.
- OPM should establish, or facilitate creation of, benchmarks for HR efficiency. The measures should be specific enough to allow for valid comparisons with like operations.

ACHIEVING MORE EFFECTIVE HUMAN RESOURCES MANAGEMENT: A STRATEGY

HR's activities should be mission-driven and value-added. Key characteristics of this model are:

- Line management is in charge of, and accountable for, HR processes.
- HR is measured by the value it adds to the organization's mission accomplishment.
- HR is a respected part of the organization's leadership.
- HR staffing, organization, technology strategy, policies and practices are developed based on the results the organization seeks.
- Corporate offices give business units (bureaus) considerable latitude to tailor their HR programs within the construct of very general policies and principles.
- HR staffs and managers develop HR competencies that enable them to apply HR principles to solve organizational problems.
- HR staffs have broad knowledge of the mission that augment a high level of expertise in HRM basics.

To achieve this new model, there must be:

- A clear vision for HRM in federal government operations. The role and expectations for HRM must be derived from legislation. Agencies should be given authority to develop human resources systems that are tailored to their cultures, missions, and the prevailing labor market norms for their occupations. Centrally controlled programs should be limited to those that are not core to missions. Accountability should be clearly stated in terms of developing and utilizing

Agency leaders must undertake a focused effort to identify and provide training on the critical competencies managers need to operate in a human resources system where there are fewer rules, tailored agency systems, expanded delegation of authority, and line management accountability for results.

human resources effectively to meet current mission and future strategic goals and should be reflected in the agency's performance management system.

- Continuity of leadership in the positions responsible for federal HRM. One approach is to have time-limited appointments for those positions and to require employment and performance contracts for senior operating executives such as those used by New Zealand.

- Line management competency in HRM. Agency leaders must undertake a focused effort to identify and provide training on the critical competencies managers need to operate in a human resources system where there are fewer rules, tailored agency systems, expanded delegation of authority, and line management accountability for results. The two critical competencies for line managers are supervisory skills and leadership skills.

- A more professional and competent human resources staff. Human resources staffs need to improve their professional reputation and competence to gain acceptance as a strategic partner. A model for HR staff development is presented in Chapter 6 of this report. HR must also rethink its hiring practices for HR professionals. Individuals with advanced degrees in business administration or an HR specialty are considered top candidates in the private sector. Also considered desirable are people who can bring practical experience in line organizations to the job.

- Measures to cope with HR staff reductions. Agencies must use various strategies to deal with the reductions in the HR staff, which generally occur at a rate greater than the reductions in the rest of the federal workforce. Among the opportunities for HR to operate more effectively with fewer resources are: management/ employee self-sufficiency, increased use of technology, the use of measurement systems to manage and focus HR activities, process improvement and reengineering, and alternative service delivery.

- Strategies that meet the needs of small agencies. Many smaller agencies do not have a dedicated policy and program staff to undertake broad developmental activities associated with transforming HRM. Small agencies may need to redirect the efforts of their HR staff from operational HR aspects by contracting out or franchising those activities, to provide consultative and strategic services to line managers.

Actions suggested to improve the performance of the federal HRM system are:

- Develop comprehensive legislative specifications that clearly outline the roles and expectations for HRM in the federal government, and give agencies the flexibility to tailor their HR systems to complement organizational cultures and missions.

- The administration and Congress should address the problems associated with the frequent turnover of individuals who manage civil servants involved in operational functions.

- Agencies' trainers should develop updated training programs for managers, employees and HR specialists to improve HRM performance at all levels. A recommended model for such a program is provided in Chapter 6.

- OPM, or a consortium of agencies, should develop a certification program to ensure a high quality HR staff throughout the government. In the initial years, certification should be used as a training needs identification tool. In future

Organizations must find better ways to recruit, develop, lead and nurture the human components of the organization who are the source of organizational knowledge and performance.

years, it should be used as a requirement for promotion to senior HR positions at grades GS-13 and above.

- As a strategy for dealing with HR staff reductions, agency leaders should continue to invest in technology to provide the infrastructure to empower employees and managers to perform more of their own HR work. In addition, agencies' HR leaders should continue to aggressively pursue opportunities to collaborate on system improvements such as the current Department of Health and Human Services project to develop "Employee Express."

- Small agencies' HR leaders should examine opportunities to franchise or contract HR operational functions to other providers while retaining the ability to perform the strategic advisor role for their agencies.

CHAPTER 1

Introduction

> *"The human resources activity must focus its resources on solving business problems, not developing programs and hoping they will be bought."*
>
> HR executive with a manufacturing company.
> Source:Frank Manley & Co.

This statement is indicative of the challenges human resources (HR) staffs face today. How can HR make itself relevant to the organizational challenges line managers face in the public and private sectors? Both sectors are undergoing an unprecedented pace of change.

> *"Already an estimated two-thirds of U.S. employees work in the services sector; and knowledge is becoming our most important product."*
>
> Peter Drucker, Post Capitalists Society

Peter Drucker's quote drives home the importance of the human factor to success in today's and tomorrow's organizations. Knowledge is brought to the organization by people. No amount of capital investment in machines and bricks and mortar will overcome a deficiency in human capital (knowledge). How we recruit, develop, lead, and nurture the human component of organizations is not simply a matter of controlling labor costs. It is a matter of investing wisely to obtain the human talent that is essential to success. In the public sector, this is especially important as the public demands increasingly sophisticated services and decreasing costs.

This report addresses the issues that are critical to developing a new paradigm for federal human resources management (HRM). Agencies participating in the National Academy of Public Administration (NAPA) HRM project were previously provided two

Knowledge is brought to the organization by people. No amount of capital investment in machines and bricks and mortar will overcome a deficiency in human capital (knowledge).

Introduction

documents that accompany this report: Human Resources Management Literature Review and Bibliography, and Innovative Approaches to HRM.

The literature review, completed in January 1995, summarizes information from 367 articles, publications, and books. These materials capture the ideas and concepts of leading thinkers in the fields of HRM and public administration. The innovative HRM practices compendium, completed in April 1995, describes the experiences of 20 leading-edge private and public organizations that are dealing with the changing role of HRM.

Another source of information is the ideas and thoughts of 50 federal managers, 49 employees, and 69 human resources experts who participated in NAPA-organized focus groups in Atlanta, Dallas, New York, San Francisco, and Washington D.C. A summary of the focus group results is provided at Appendix B. The purpose of the focus groups was to obtain employee input concerning the current state of human resources management in the federal government and changes needed to ensure that the human contribution to organizational success is optimized.

Finally, NAPA staff held discussion sessions with small agency managers and HR specialists to better understand the unique needs of small agencies. A report summarizing these meetings is provided at Appendix C.

The question of transferability of innovative HRM concepts from the private sector to the federal government is fundamental to effective HR reinvention efforts. Many experts express the view that private sector models have limited utility in the federal setting due to unique federal HRM features such as: the merit system; employee due process rights; veterans preference; unique reduction-in-force requirements; and the hostile environment in which the system operates, including intense press scrutiny and the political value of bureaucrat bashing. These factors are considered to be a practical barrier to innovation and improvement, but also serve as a psychological barrier to the risk taking necessary to break the current paradigm that defines the federal employment system.

Fundamental changes in federal personnel work which will enable optimum transfer of private sector best practices will require legislation.

It is true that fundamental changes in federal personnel work which will enable optimum transfer of private sector best practices will require legislation. The current federal human resources system was originally designed in the 1920s and severely limits federal managers' ability to make many of the changes taking place in the more progressive parts of the private sector. The NAPA HRM Project Panel, with input from participating agencies, will outline the legislative changes needed to provide additional flexibility to align HRM systems with mission requirements. In the meantime, agencies can take advantage of private sector best practices to:

- Make HRM a strategic partner with agency leadership;
- Use Government Performance and Results Act (GPRA) strategic plans and National Performance Review (NPR) performance contracts to align HRM activities with mission results;
- Implement robust measurement systems to determine how well HRM values, goals and strategies are being implemented;
- Develop training and career management programs to prepare line managers and HR staffs for new and expanded roles;

- Reengineer HR processes to eliminate non-value added steps;
- Invest in information technology to improve service and reduce costs of the HR system;
- Organize HR staffs around reengineered processes and customer service requirements; and
- Implement greater accountability for HRM by beginning to remove those barriers that are within agencies' current authority.

What Have We Learned?

- Leading companies give their business units considerable autonomy to develop approaches to managing their people in a way that fits their business environments and cultures. The notion of tight central controls on most human resources activities has been replaced by delegated authority and accountability for results for effective management of people. **This challenges the traditional notion of the federal government as a single employer, and the value of lock-step consistency at the expense of effectiveness.** The time has arrived for greater agency autonomy to develop their own human resources systems, guided by merit principles.

- **Line managers manage human resources and are accountable for results.** Leading organizations have well-defined performance measurement systems. Line managers are measured in terms of their contribution to business success, customer satisfaction, and contributions to the human capacity within the organization. Contributions in these areas are often measured by employee surveys and 360-degree appraisal systems, and are a major factor in compensation decisions. NAPA did not find a similar condition in federal organizations. The NPR clearly states the case for such accountability, but action has been lacking. Legislation to simplify processes is needed to empower managers, and it is not in place.

- **Human resources in leading organizations is becoming a strategic partner with senior line management.** This has required a rethinking of the competencies that are essential to success. The driver for any human resources activity is the mission/business objectives. HR sits at the table and participates when decisions are made about business plans, goals, and objectives. It adds value by assisting and advising line managers who create and adapt HR programs, policies, and processes which advance the objectives of the organization. HR serves as a change agent to raise organizational awareness of the relationship between HR and mission accomplishment.

- **The strategic partner role requires a new set of competencies for HR professionals.** While knowledge of the mainline HR business — recruitment; compensation; training and development; organizational development; employee and labor relations — is still important, those competencies are the baseline upon which other skills such as business knowledge, the image to function as a member of the senior team, and consultancy, have been added. Achieving the stature as a strategic partner is not an easy matter. It requires a combination of competence to make a value-added contribution to the organization, an organizational structure which ensures direct access to decision makers, top management commitment and vision, and a recognition that people are a vital element of organizational success.

The strategic partner role requires a new set of competencies for HR professionals.

Introduction

- **Employees are being required to assume a greater role for managing their careers** and managing their benefit programs. Modern technology is taking this capability to the workforce where employees can perform for themselves more of the work which was previously performed in the HR office. This same technology is providing additional capability to managers to perform their HR functions, and to have access to workforce data which are needed for decision making. As a result, HR staff are being freed up to perform more value-added work as strategic partners, consultants, and advisors.

The remainder of this report provides a suggested strategy to achieve a new role for federal HR operations. Questions that will be addressed include:

- What **outcomes** are expected from the HRM process? How do merit system principles fit into and contribute to a focus on organizational results? Does the current process for achieving a merit system in the federal government contribute or detract from organizational performance?
- What are line management's and HR staff's **roles** for successfully engaging the workforce to achieve organizational goals? How should **accountability** for line managers, employees, and HR staff members be defined and implemented?
- What **measures** are available to determine whether human resources objectives have been accomplished? What measures should be used for managers, employees, and human resources staffs?
- What **changes** need to be made in the current federal human resources system to more effectively deploy and utilize the federal workforce to serve the American public's interests?
- What are the **options for delivering HR services** and what are the advantages and disadvantages of each? Can the dual goals of increased efficiency and improved effectiveness be achieved?
- How should HR staff **organize** to ensure that HR issues are appropriately integrated into organizational planning, management, and operational processes, and that line managers receive essential HR services?
- What are the implications of changes in HR roles and responsibilities for managers, HR staffs and employees? What **competencies**, technology, recruitment, career paths, training/education of line managers, employees, and HR staffs are needed to cope in this new environment?

CHAPTER 2

Aligning HRM System With Organizational Results

> *"Concentrating on outcomes will also keep you from falling in love with a particular methodology. Or to put it another way, you're less likely to waste time, energy, and other resources on low-payoff work routines if your real passion is for reaching results."*
>
> Price Pritchett 1994

ORGANIZATIONAL GOALS AND DESIRED RESULTS DRIVE HRM PROGRAMS AND PROCESSES

Ultimately, the results HRM processes achieve must be synonymous with organizational success. Recent studies in the private sector have established a linkage between progressive HRM practices and the firm's financial performance. These findings make a strong case for HR to concentrate its efforts on those activities that add value to organizational performance. The activities found to contribute to organizational performance include such mainline HR programs as employee selection, job design, performance appraisals, promotion systems, employee surveys, incentive systems, and labor-management participation programs. More detail on these findings is provided in the NAPA literature review.

Management's challenge is to connect HRM work to mission requirements. This requires careful analysis of the mission outcomes desired and the human factors necessary to achieve successful results. Fitz-enz (Human Value Management) suggests that this task can be directly addressed by asking such basic questions as:

- What is the problem?
- What is the reason for the problem?
- Why is it a problem? Cost? Time? Quality?
- What would be a workable solution?

The activities found to contribute to organizational performance include such mainline HR programs as employee selection, job design, performance appraisals, promotion systems, employee surveys, incentive systems, and labor-management participation programs.

Aligning HRM System With Organizational Results

Xerox has aggressively pursued the linkage of human resources to company strategic goals. The company has established global growth and productivity as primary business goals. HR determined that their mission is to facilitate productivity and employee satisfaction in ways that will contribute value to achieving these two business goals. For example, through analysis it was determined that increased productivity could be achieved by providing new skills to employees. In consultation with Xerox managers, HR determined how the programs designed to provide employees new skills (training, education, self-development, compensation, communication and performance feedback) could be better focused to contribute to increased productivity. A similar approach was used to determine how HR processes such as compensation, rewards/recognition, performance feedback and succession planning could be used to improve employees' customer focus — thereby contributing to global growth. Xerox did not just deliver HRM programs and processes, but rather designed tailored interventions that ensured that business goals were the primary drivers of HR priorities and activities.

The federal government is often challenged by the lack of a clear set of goals. Congress passed GPRA in 1993 to improve the effectiveness and performance of federal programs by establishing a system to set goals and measure performance. GPRA requires that federal agencies establish 5-year strategic plans, identify goals and describe how the agency intends to achieve those goals through its activities, including its human capital, information, and other resources. GPRA allows agencies to propose waivers to administrative requirements. In return for the waivers, agencies are to be held accountable for achieving the promised performance improvements. This allows agencies to propose flexibilities to improve HR programs and processes to more closely align HRM with organizational goals and strategic plans. A review of a sample of agency plans submitted under GPRA pilot tests does not demonstrate that agencies have fully recognized the human component of improving organizational performance. Nor do those agreements between agency heads and the President, which have been developed so far in response to the NPR, reflect clear emphasis on the linkage between effective human resources management and achievement of mission objectives.

> "Some of the states were beginning to align their HR systems to better ensure that the systems support line managers in their efforts to achieve statewide and agency goals."

The U.S. General Accounting Office (GAO) recently examined six states that had implemented GPRA-type legislation with provisions for results-oriented management reforms such as; strategic planning, performance measurement, and alignment of management systems with results goals. This review indicated that, "Some of the states were beginning to align their HR systems to better ensure that the systems support line managers in their efforts to achieve statewide and agency goals." Specifically; Florida, Minnesota, North Carolina, and Oregon were cited for their efforts to align their human resources systems with organizational goals. One general conclusion is that the move to relax some personnel requirements is in the interest of achieving government program results. Specific actions states took to better align human resources policies with organizational goals included changing appraisal systems and streamlining staffing rules and procedures. These actions lend support to those who argue that the time has arrived to jettison the notion of the federal government as a single employer with a uniform set of policies that must be stretched and bent to fit all situations regardless of the diversity of mission and goals.

Florida provided state managers with more flexibility to modify HRM policies and processes to facilitate desired program results. Through pilot programs, state agencies were allowed to act outside of Florida's normal personnel statutory requirements. This goes further than GPRA, which only permits waivers of nonstatutory administrative provisions. Florida agencies have the authority to establish their own personnel classification and pay plans and transfer funds and budget authority internally without prior approval from the Executive Office of the Governor. Flexibilities are being used to: change dispute resolution processes; adopt family friendly policies such as flexible hours, days and work sites; provide raises not tied to promotion; and use classification broad-banding systems. Significantly, agencies are encouraged to experiment in the name of achieving results. No "one-size-fits-all" approach is presumed, and consistency is not valued above service to the public.

> *"The personnel system often concentrates on inputs and ignores outcomes, limits managers' flexibility, hides the true costs of programs and encourages waste."*
> Florida Governor's Commission for Government by the People

The issue of how to better align human resources with organizational goals often runs head-on into long-established merit system requirements. For example, GAO cites the Minnesota Commission on Reform and Efficiency (CORE) report, which critiques the Minnesota HR system. The system was established in 1939 to ensure stability and combat problems of patronage and inequitably applied personnel polices. CORE noted that this system had grown too complex and unresponsive to meet the needs of government and the people it serves. In a sense, the rights of applicants had become more valued than the needs of taxpayers and state managers for a responsive human resources system.

These conclusions are similar to those noted by Ingraham and Rosenbloom in their paper, The State of Merit in the Federal Government. They conclude: "The current system essentially assumes that public managers must be coerced into meritorious behavior; there is no presumption that, left to their own skills and conscience, members of the federal service will nevertheless pursue quality and effective service."

> *"All of us together – Republican and Democrat alike – must totally remake the federal government, to change the very way it thinks, the way it does business, the way it treats its citizens."*
> Newt Gingrich, April 7, 1995

FEDERAL MANAGERS', EMPLOYEES', AND HUMAN RESOURCES SPECIALISTS' VIEWS ON HR RESULTS

NAPA convened focus groups of federal managers, employees and human resources specialists to discuss what outcomes should be expected from an ideal HR system. The summary results reflecting common themes from the sessions are shown in Table 1.

Aligning HRM System With Organizational Results

Part of the challenge of creating reinvented HRM systems will be to change the expectations of all the players.

TABLE 1

Expected Outcomes From an HRM System

Employees	Managers	HR Specialists
▪ Trained Managers ▪ Caring/Human Touch ▪ Simpler System ▪ More Flexibility	▪ Local Technical HR Support ▪ A Strategic Plan (Direction) ▪ Simple Hiring & Classification ▪ Flexibility-Fewer Rules	▪ Timely & Accurate Information ▪ On-Site Service Delivery ▪ Fairness & Equity ▪ Quality Employees

These comments suggest that stakeholders in the focus group discussions did not view the HRM process in terms of its contribution to agency goals and objectives. Rather the tendency was to couch expectations in terms of processes.

> *"To reinvent HRM, we must redefine accountability in terms of results – and we must do so within the context of decentralization, simplicity, flexibility, and substantially increased delegations of authority."*

National Performance Review Accompanying Report on Human Resources.

Specific actions to improve the alignment of HRM with agency goals and strategies are:

- Use GPRA strategic plans and NPR performance agreements with the president as vehicles to link tailored approaches to HRM with improved mission results.
- Actively involve HR staffs in developing GPRA strategic plans and NPR performance agreements which identify specific HR initiatives designed to enhance achievement of mission results.
- Congress should permit agencies to waive statutory requirements as they develop tailored approaches to HRM if such waivers would advance agency program results, within the context of basic principles such as equal employment opportunity (EEO), merit hiring and promotion, and health and safety programs. Oversight of agency waivers should be provided by means of normal Office of Management and Budget (OMB) and congressional program reviews.
- The Office of Personnel Management (OPM) should establish, or facilitate creation of, a clearinghouse of best practices that agencies can use to design approaches to more closely align HRM with agency strategy and program goals.

CHAPTER 3

HRM Roles, Systems and Accountability

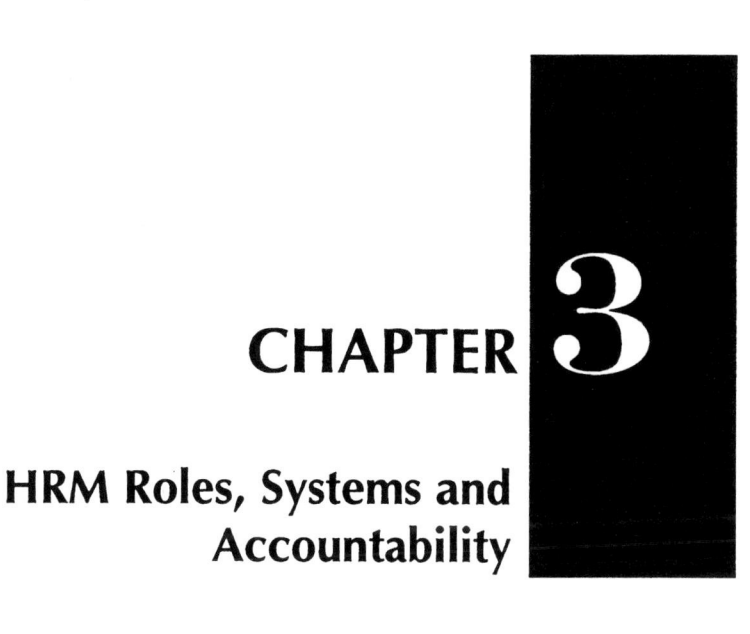

> *HR executives are increasingly involved in strategic organization and business issues.*
>
> Frank B. Manley 1994

HR AS A STRATEGIC PARTNER

Human resources managers must be involved in strategic management issues, as a partner with line management, if they are to align HR programs and processes with mission goals and results. NAPA's analysis of organizations with innovative HRM practices found that involvement in strategic issues is a characteristic of leading firms. Companies such as Hewlett-Packard, AT&T, and Xerox, and public sector organizations such as Washington State and the City of Charlotte, have achieved or are well along with the transition to including HR leadership as a member of the strategic team. These organizations' approaches are described in detail in the compendium of innovative practices. Why has the HR leadership in these organizations achieved acceptance as a strategic partner? Figure 1 lists some common elements that are characteristic of HR's involvement at the strategic level. These elements are a combination

FIGURE 1

Drivers of HR Involvement as a Strategic Partner

- People issues are a key to achieving organization goals and a competitive advantage.

- Major organizational changes (such as downsizing, reengineering, reorganization, TQM, mergers & acquisitions, and use of self directed work teams) are dependent on successful HRM strategies.

- HR interventions require knowledge of a body of knowledge in the HR profession — not just anyone can do HR work at this level.

- The HR organization has prepared itself to accomplish the strategic role by developing competence in the business as well as HR specializations.

NAPA's analysis of organizations with innovative HRM practices found that involvement in strategic issues is a characteristic of leading firms.

of insights and actions by senior line managers and action taken by the HR leadership to prepare itself to serve in an expanded role.

What is the strategic HR role? When HR is a strategic partner it is involved with the leadership team when major decisions that affect the future of the organization are discussed and debated. HR's specific contribution to this discussion is to ensure that people issues associated with achieving future organizational goals are understood and discussed. Examples of the types of issues HR might discuss include: the availability of needed skills in the company or labor market; the impact of skills changes on compensation costs; the costs and impacts of downsizing; the need for additional investments in training and education; the need to address issues in a labor-management partnership forum; and the need for a planned approach to merging cultures of different organizations being brought together through acquisition or reorganization. While some might argue that HR would do these things anyway, as a strategic partner HR is at the table when the decision is made, rather than reacting to a decision. This participation ensures a clear understanding of goals and context. Working with management, HR develops and deploys approaches and programs to align people management with mission goals and results. Further discussion of the strategic role is included in the literature review that accompanies this report.

Infrastructure conditions are important to HR's ability to function as a strategic partner. These include:

- HR's reporting relationship must to be to a member of the top management team. Many HR leaders from the leading edge companies report directly to the Chief Executive Officer (CEO).
- HR must have access to information technology (hardware, software, telecommunications, and databases) that facilitate sophisticated analyses of workforce status and trends.
- HR must make a considerable investment to develop the skills needed to serve in this role. More detail on the types of skills needed is provided in Chapter 6 of this report.

OTHER HR ROLES

The emergence of the strategic role for HR receives much attention in current literature. However, there are other enduring roles that will likely continue. There is a move to transfer much of the HR administrative work to line managers and employees through use of information technology, but to a large extent that is still on the "to do" list. In the meantime, HR needs to accomplish this work in an efficient and effective manner. Two of the innovative practices firms NAPA interviewed, Air Products and Intel, identified HR work with three categories or "buckets".

- The first bucket is the **administrative role,** which contains high-volume, routine processing-type activities. Examples of this type of work are health benefits and other benefit programs, such as employee investment plans. Outputs from this work are documentation and information. While these duties tend to be somewhat routine, doing this work well is often a precondition for being accepted to serve the more substantive roles defined in the other buckets. This work is typically performed by HR employees who are specialists in a relatively narrow field such as benefit administration. Many companies are focusing their HR reengineering efforts on this area to redesign processes and then provide automated systems that make it possible for others outside HR to provide self-service. The goal is to reduce HR staffing and costs to perform these functions and free the HR staff to do other work that will add value to the mission.

- The second bucket are primarily **advisory and consultative** duties provided to line managers to help them address current business needs, either solving a problem or making an improvement. The primary difference between this role and the strategic role is the focus on current issues with known facts instead of addressing future conditions. This work is increasingly performed by generalists who know a broad range of HR topics and possess change-agent skills to facilitate organizational development initiatives. The particular competence that makes the advisor valuable is the ability to integrate HR functional knowledge to design alternative solutions to business problems from which the line manager can choose. Participants in the NAPA focus groups all identified the advisory or consultant role as a primary requirement for the future. Considerable information on this role is provided in the literature review and the compendium of innovative practices.

- The third bucket is the **strategic role** discussed previously.

LINE MANAGEMENT'S ROLE AND ACCOUNTABILITY FOR MANAGING PEOPLE

It was an accepted principle in the private sector firms visited during this project that line managers are responsible for HRM. Some noteworthy examples are AT&T, Hewlett-Packard, Intel and Xerox. Some public sector organizations are also moving in this direction including the State of Washington, Canada's National Defense Department, and the City of Charlotte, N.C.

Barriers to a Greater Line Management Role

While there seems to be acceptance of the principle that federal line managers should assume a greater role in managing

FIGURE 2

Barriers to Federal Line Managers Control of HRM

- The current federal HRM system is too complex.
- Procedures which implement the HR system are often focused on goals other than mission results.
- Information technology used for federal HRM tends to be focused on processing actions rather than providing tools which will enable line managers to perform HRM duties efficiently.
- Lack of clarity regarding mission results being sought makes it difficult to align HR with issues relevant to the mission.
- Centralized control of most substantive HR policy makes it difficult to tailor HRM to mission needs and take advantage of best practices outside the federal government.
- Managers have not received sufficient training on HR principles and techniques.
- The federal culture discourages risk taking.
- There is a lack of leadership continuity due to frequent turnover of top managers.

The particular competence that makes the advisor valuable is the ability to integrate HR functional knowledge to design alternative solutions to business problems.

HRM Roles, Systems and Accountability

their employees, it has not happened to the extent that it occurs in the progressive parts of the private sector. NPR documents the intent to achieve a greater role for line managers. Why has this transition not occurred? What are the barriers and what must occur for line managers to be able to assume a greater role in managing people who report to them? The insert in the Figure 2 identifies some of the barriers that were frequently mentioned.

STRATEGIES FOR ADDRESSING BARRIERS

The removal of barriers to line management's assumption of a greater role in and more accountability for managing the federal workforce is a fundamental issue that is a precondition for major HRM improvements. The following are actions that are important to achieving this goal.

Simplify and Decentralize the HR System

If managers are to be responsible for HRM, the systems must be simple, easy to understand and use, and accessible. This point was made emphatically during focus group discussions with federal line managers. They do not have the time or the knowledge to assume a greater role given the current rule-intensive system. Real change in these processes will require legislative action that empowers line organizations to design their own HRM programs and policies. Beyond that, agencies must also look at their tendency to substitute departmental control for central agency control as has happened in some agencies in the past when OPM has delegated authority to agencies. Many agencies have recently taken action to reduce the number of internal policies, which should be helpful.

Increased Use of Information Technology

For decades, federal agencies have used computers to support personnel and payroll functions. What is missing? A number of changes have occurred that makes the need for an aggressive and coordinated technology strategy critical to successful management of the federal workforce.

First, staffing reductions among human resources staff and line managers have eliminated the ability to use brute force substitution of labor for technology to solve personnel processing problems. Asking already-burdened managers to assume a greater role in the current system is not acceptable.

Second, managers recognize that existing transaction processing systems, while important, are not sufficient to support management's need for user-friendly systems that can be operated by existing (or hopefully) fewer administrative staff members in line organizations. Managers need new tools that provide workforce information directly for planning and decision making. Third, it is increasingly understood that there are many benefits to putting automated systems in the hands of employees to do some of their own personnel work. The Department of Health and Human Services (HHS) led initiative to develop "Employee Express" is a good example of this.

Finally, recent HRM-related software developments have made it possible to customize automation approaches without the major investment required for a tailored mainframe program. With the advent of client-server technology, robust applications and information can be delivered to managers' desktops. Telephone response systems

Agencies must also look at their tendency to substitute departmental control for central agency control.

make it possible to implement user-friendly systems for benefit administration and staffing applications. "Software agents" make it possible for computers to answer phones, generate forms and letters, and move information to the location where it is needed for planning and decision making. New applications permit managers to obtain lists of rated candidates, describe and classify positions, and send employees to training all without involving the servicing HR office.

Most of the organizations NAPA interviewed have made extensive use of technology to perform HR activities. Automated systems have allowed HR departments to transform themselves from transaction processors to advisors, consultants, and strategic partners. More important, technology has given managers the wherewithal to manage their workforce. NAPA's review of federal HR systems development indicates a high level of activity. In some instances, such as "Employee Express," there is a coordinated approach. In most cases, however, it appears that there is a very limited degree of technology transfer among agencies. This may be because there is no clearinghouse for HR technology developments. Another concern is whether line managers participate in developing systems requirements. If managers are to "own" HR, they must actively participate in the development of HR systems.

Improving HRM Focus on Results

As discussed in Chapter 2, agencies need to use GPRA strategic plans and the NPR performance contracts as a basis to better align HR programs with mission goals. This will create a greater incentive for line managers to get more engaged in HRM. Mission results will be clearer, as will the relationship of HRM to achieving those results.

Management Training

Managers will need considerable training to assume an expanded HRM role. A conceptual training model for managers is described in Chapter 6 of this report.

Addressing Resistance to Cultural Change

Many pundits have noted that federal managers are risk-adverse. Reasons given for this perceived condition include an imbalance in the risk-reward equation. Federal managers fail to see that the benefits of taking risks are likely to yield a significant reward, as is sometimes the case in the private sector. On the other hand, taking a risk and failing may well result in public humiliation and termination of career opportunities. Intense and scandal-driven press coverage of public business is almost certain to ensure that even minor failures receive broad dissemination to the public.

The nature of politics has driven some elected officials and candidates to highlight mistakes in governmental performance. Yet, being willing to take risks is a fundamental condition for getting managers to accept a greater role in and accountability for HRM. To facilitate successful transition to the new role, it is necessary that inspectors general, Congress, other elected officials, and senior career leaders create an environment that is more forgiving of honest mistakes made in the quest for improved mission results. At the same time, federal managers must be willing to not only reward risk taking, but enforce consequences when that is appropriate. Doing so is as much a matter of will as system barriers.

HRM Roles, Systems and Accountability

Leadership Continuity

Problems associated with frequent turnover of political leadership are described in Chapter 6. This is also an important factor in establishing conditions favorable to greater roles for career line organization leaders in workforce management.

ACCOUNTABILITY FOR HRM RESULTS

One of the topics frequently debated in the context of reforming the federal civil service is the matter of accountability. Those opposed to significant change in the current system argue that any major devolution of authority must be accompanied by a rigorous system of oversight to ensure that merit system principles are not compromised as managers respond to other goals. Discussing this topic from a theoretical perspective has defied consensus. However, review of the practical experience of public-private sector organizations that have devolved authority to line managers suggests the following:

Compliance with policies is more probable if HRM programs provide flexibility to rationalize people management with mission goals and results.

FIGURE 3

Conditions for Establishing HRM Accountability

- Establish clear HRM goals tied to desired mission results. The number of goals should be limited to avoid loss of focus.
- Focus on values rather than detailed rules. This will provide a flexible context for managers to accomplish mission results while supporting government-wide values.
- Provide adequate training and information so that it is clear what managers are accountable for. Use multiple channels of communication to enhance understanding.
- Demonstrate top line management leadership by example. Leading companies such as AT&T, Xerox, and Hewlett-Packard have demonstrated the importance of top management leadership of HRM values initiatives.
- Enforce consequences. Willful violations of values must be addressed in a clear and forthright manner, and outstanding support of values should be rewarded.
- Measurement systems must be in place to determine whether HRM values are taking hold in the organization.

- The vast majority of line managers and HR staff are reliable and trustworthy. Among the experiences that support this are those of Washington State, New Zealand, and the City of Charlotte, NC.
- Compliance with policies is more probable if HRM programs provide flexibility to rationalize people management with mission goals and results.
- There is a positive correlation between the simplicity of the HRM system and compliance with the system.
- In the past, when rigorous central oversight was provided, there were still instances of merit systems abuses. The emphasis on compliance also displaced the relationship of HRM to mission results in favor of a culture that adhered to procedures and documentation requirements.

If managers are to be fully accountable for mission results, they need to have authority over key management systems, such as budget and human resources. This is feasible in the public sector as demonstrated by the experience in New Zealand. Performance management systems must clearly tie human

TABLE 2

Distribution of HRM Accountability Between HR and Line Managers

Manager's HRM Accountability	HR's Accountability
• Defining and communicating desired HRM outcomes and values to employees and servicing HR organization. • Providing visible support for values — lead by examples. • Delegating authority to subordinate managers commensurate with responsibilities. • Measuring HRM results. • Applying consequences when values are supported or violated. • Achieving performance goals. • Designing performance management systems that clearly tie HRM with achieving organizational mission.	• Understanding outcomes and values required by line organization and designing HR support that meets those requirements. • Providing strategies and accurate and timely advice to line managers. • Executing HR operational functions in an efficient and effective manner to minimize costs. • Serving as a role model for the organization's people values. • Measuring HR's contribution to mission results. • Achieving HR performance goals. • Ensuring that the performance management system works.

resources management with achieving the organization's mission. Leading-edge organizations, such as Hewlett-Packard, AT&T and Xerox, have established performance measurement systems that hold managers accountable for the productivity and satisfaction of staffs.

Figure 3 presents suggested guidelines for agencies to ensure that an environment exists that fosters concern for accountability for positive HRM practices.

What About HR's Accountability?

Making managers accountable for their workforce does not absolve HR staffs of any responsibility and accountability. On the contrary, it more clearly focuses expectations about what HR delivers and the utility of those services to achieving mission results. Table 2 suggests a likely distribution of accountability between line managers and HR staffs.

Employee's Role in HR System

Reductions in the number of line managers and HR specialists as a result of NPR and other initiatives to reduce the size and scope of government will cause a change in the roles of employees and their relationships with their line managers. Employees will need to be more responsible for their own performance, career development, benefit administration, and the accuracy of their personnel data. Organizations interviewed spoke of changing their contract with employees. Some noted that hard work, commitment and high-level performance could no longer guarantee employment with the organization. Employees are being asked to assume responsibility for their employability.

Given the realities of future resources levels, agencies should begin to facilitate this cultural change by working with unions in the spirit of partnership and clearly explaining to employees the need for greater individual responsibility.

HRM Roles, Systems and Accountability

The organization will provide the resources for employees to stay employable, but the impetus must come from the employees. Employees are also being asked to assume a greater role for performing activities traditionally performed by HR offices. Examples include self-service programs for health benefits, investment programs, and application procedures for vacancies. The HR staff is still there to deal with the exceptional cases, but routine issues are the employees' responsibility. These changes, if carried forward into the public sector, will fundamentally alter how the federal government has traditionally dealt with employees. In some instances, this approach will conflict with existing union contracts which prescribe a more parental approach to employees. Given the realities of future resources levels, agencies should begin to facilitate this cultural change by working with unions in the spirit of partnership and clearly explaining to employees the need for greater individual responsibility for benefit administration and career management. Also, automated systems should be developed and deployed to the worksite so that employees have the necessary tools to perform this new role.

Agencies can improve HRM by:

- Taking action to establish and reinforce HR's role as a strategic partner through involvement in discussion, formulation, and deployment of mission strategies and goals;
- Making an investment to develop HR staff competence to function in all role dimensions discussed in this report;
- Establishing and enforcing line managers leadership of, and accountability for, HRM;
- Creating an environment that mitigates the barriers to accountability by simplifying and decentralizing the HR system, increasing the use of information technology, improving HRM focus on results, providing management training, creating a culture that tolerates risk, and promoting management continuity; and
- Initiating action to build greater employee self-reliance for their employability, for ensuring the accuracy of their personnel data, and administering their benefits package.

CHAPTER 4

Structuring the Organization to Provide HRM Services

After an organization has defined its philosophy for how it wants to manage people and the role of its HR office, it can develop service delivery models and an organizational structure that maximize the organization's ability to achieve the desired results. The major staff reductions planned for federal HR and management employees makes the selection of efficient models a priority.

Managing people is a complex business. In the federal sector it is made more difficult by the legislation, regulations and policies that determine the HR environment. This environment has resulted in significant specialization in the HR functional areas and has created HR organizations and service delivery models aligned along functional lines. To provide more integrated programs and services, HR needs to move away from these narrow, specialized ways of doing business.

Reengineering HR activities and practices will realign HR along process lines. The NAPA panel envisions that departments and agencies will do whatever they can to reengineer their HR work. Even without reengineering, HR departments can reorganize the work they perform to provide for most coherent planning and service delivery. A joint project by Canada's Human Resource Policy Branch and the Personnel Renewal Council proposed a model that "clusters" HR functions to improve service delivery. This model was not meant to be all-inclusive but can help organizations define their core HR functional requirements and assess delivery options.

Detailed information of what is included in each cluster is included in Attachment C.

The major staff reductions planned for federal HR and management employees makes the selection of efficient models a priority.

FIGURE 4

Factors Affecting the Choice of HR Service Delivery Models

- Organizational culture
- Organizational size
- Mission of the department or agency
- Geographic dispersion of the workforce
- Resource availability
- The extent to which processes are automated
- Client expectations

Structuring the Organization to Provide HRM Services

HR reengineering activities need to be guided by three key question: does it need to be done?; can it be outsourced to achieve cost savings or improve service?; and if kept in-house, how can it be done better?

FIGURE 5

Proposed "Clusters" of HR Functions
■ Sustainable organizational health ■ Continuous learning strategies ■ Organizational analysis and design ■ Employment strategies ■ Compensation management ■ Management development and support ■ Management of the HR function

HR reengineering activities need to be guided by three key questions:

- Does it need to be done?
- Can it be outsourced to achieve cost savings or improve service?
- If kept in-house, how can it be done better?

DOES IT NEED TO BE DONE?

If an HR activity does not add value to the organization, perhaps it should not done at all. Many HR activities are dictated by legal or regulatory requirements. Where they are not, HR departments should ask whether activities, which were established in a different era to solve different problems, could be eliminated. HR's customers need to be active participants in this process. The customer should make the decision about what HR activities and practices to eliminate.

Participants in the focus groups suggested that a number of HR activities be discarded including:

- Many reporting requirements.
- Monitoring/enforcing flex-time and "core hour" rules.
- Testing and registers.
- Panels and best-qualified determinations.
- Third-level supervisory complaint resolution step.
- HR involvement in the performance rating process.
- Performance appraisals.

CAN HUMAN RESOURCES ACTIVITIES BE OUTSOURCED?

There is no "one best way" for an organization to structure itself to deliver HR services. The clusters developed in the Canadian project (see Figure 5) emphasize the lack of a "one size fits all" model. One of the initial steps in structuring HR within an organization is to determine whether HR services should be performed in-house or outsourced — contracted out to private firms or "franchised" to other federal agencies.

While the concepts of internal service delivery and contracting out are familiar to most federal managers, so-called "franchising" may be less well-known. Franchised functions or services are those performed by a "lead provider" (usually another federal agency) that can recover costs for services provided to others.

---

[1] "Guidelines for Determining HR Functions and Delivery Options" developed as a mutual project by Canada's Human Resource Policy Branch and the Personnel Renewal Council. September 1993.

TABLE 3

Criteria to Decide Where Human Resources Services Should be Provided

Service Delivery Method	Criteria for Using This Method
• Internal	• Function or service requires intimate understanding of the mission, business, culture, values, priorities, structure, constraints and opportunities of the parent organization. Functions usually are strategic in nature or require a fundamental appreciation for these issues in day-to-day client interaction and services delivery.
• Contracting Out	• Services are of a specialized nature, such that it is not feasible or cost effective to maintain internal expertise. Service standards and priority of action can be customized.
• Franchising	• Similar kinds of services needed across customer organizations lend themselves to a sole provider who can tailor some aspects to individual organizations.

Organizations need to decide where services can most effectively be provided. Table 3 offers criteria to consider in making the decision.[1]

The focus group participants developed a long list of HR activities that are candidates for contracting or franchising. A few participants believed that all HR activities belong on the list. Many of the organizations NAPA visited contract or franchise out HR services. HR organizations are looking closely at what business they want to be in and outsourcing work that is not core to meeting business goals if contractors can perform as effectively for less. Activities being outsourced in the private sector include benefits administration, investment plan (401K) administration, service-award administration, relocation services, fitness center management, payroll, and administrative support tasks. In the federal sector, several agencies contract with the Department of Agriculture's National Finance Center for payroll services and personnel systems support. Many also contract for training services, employee assistance programs and health screening services.

AN EXAMPLE OF SELECTING A MIX OF IN-HOUSE, FRANCHISING AND CONTRACTING OUT

The Canadian project model for providing the services in the HR functional clusters they proposed is presented in Table 4. For six of the clusters (management of the HR is not included), the model suggests one option for performing HR activities in-house, franchising or contracting out.

IN-HOUSE SERVICE DELIVERY MODELS

For services provided in-house, NAPA found a variety of service delivery approaches that can best be described along a continuum from totally centralized to totally

TABLE 4

A Proposed Service Delivery Model for HR Activities

	Delivery Options		
	Internal	**Franchised**	**Contracted Out**
Sustainable Organizational Health	▪ Labor-management philosophy and policy ▪ Sick leave management strategies ▪ Health and safety standards ▪ Employee assistance programs ▪ Incentives and recognition ▪ Redress Systems	▪ Investigation of health and safety complaints ▪ Employee assistance programs ▪ Harassment investigations	▪ Investigations on urgent or priority complaints ▪ Automated system development and/or maintenance of automated systems re: adjudication and legal decisions ▪ Employee assistance programs
Continuous Learning Strategies	▪ Developing training and development policies for the organization ▪ Leadership/cultural intervention strategies ▪ Organizational development priorities ▪ Strategic organizational training priorities ▪ Evaluating learning effectiveness ▪ Distance learning systems and methodologies (perhaps with external consultant design assistance)	▪ Common training: management, stress, consulting skills, negotiating skills ▪ Developing needs analysis and validation instruments ▪ Literacy surveys and training strategies	▪ Designing and delivering customized programs (perhaps using internal subject matter experts)
Organizational Analysis and Design	▪ Analyzing departmental structural options ▪ Analyzing cost-effective options ▪ Organizational design (geographic, vertical, horizontal relationships) ▪ Job description writing (dependent upon changes to classification or compensation system or the nature of the organization)	▪ Job description writing ▪ Classifying jobs	▪ Urgent situations for writing job descriptions ▪ Consultant advice on developing organizational design options or on conducting the surveys required for organization analysis

TABLE 4, continued

A Proposed Service Delivery Model for HR Activities

	Delivery Options		
	Internal	**Franchised**	**Contracted Out**
Employment Strategies	• Employee strategy development • Staffing policy and selection of resourcing options • Performance management system • Workforce modeling (based upon attrition, labor market and workforce profiles, forecasted organizational change requirements) • Support to department HRM committee	• Sensitization training and diversity management training • Local advertising, marketing, retraining for common forecasted job requirements, counseling employees, workforce modeling services • Recruiting for common requirements • Staffing transactions	• "Just-in-time" workforce sensitization or diversity acceptance training • Developing career management automated support systems
Compensation Management	• Compensation equity policy and strategies • Developing compensation packages for employees in contracting out situations	• Pre-retirement planning and training	• Delivering compensation support services to employees • Developing competency-based or multi-skilling compensation options
Management Development and Support	• Feeder group management/ identification of high performing employees • Executive staffing and identifying development needs • Performance management system • Mentoring system for high performing employees, special program participants • Compensation policies for executives and equivalents • Administering executive transition policy	• Leadership training	• Out placement services • Counseling (lifestyle balance, stress) • Survey of executive support needs/ expectations

decentralized. Depending on the service provided, organizations offer them at a number of places along the continuum.

Routine Processing Activities

Transaction-based activities, which are generally administrative and routine in nature (the "first bucket"), are increasingly being automated and moved to a shared-services delivery model. Service centers perform such common activities as benefits administration, compensation and pay processing, training, and records management. They process the paperwork and provide consulting advice related to administrative transactions. These operations are supported by sophisticated information technology, often using telephone response systems (available 24 hours a day) and networks and telecommunications reaching all employees.

Structural Considerations

Some organizations have chosen to have regional service centers. Others have chosen to have one service center that services the entire country.

- Because of resource constraints, Apple has centralized at the corporate level several HR functions that are common across business units. HR specialists are responsible for Apple University, compensation and benefits, planning, multicultural and affirmative action activities, and corporate employee relations. The central services offices formulate policy for their functional areas.

- DoD created the Civilian Personnel Management Service (CPMS) to deliver selected services from a single point at the DoD level:
    - Complaint investigation
    - Classification appeals
    - Wage setting
    - Injury and unemployment compensation
    - Pay and benefits information
    - Policy support

In addition, CPMS coordinates DoD and the armed services' efforts in the areas of:
- Information systems
- Workplace reengineering
- Business management

The military departments and Defense agencies have begun a process to regionalize operating personnel offices in the field. The projections are for 23 servicing units, or Service Centers, to provide personnel processing on a regional basis within the various services and agencies.

- At Hewlett-Packard, personnel is providing shared services in some regions of the country. For example, most personnel services for the 19 operating divisions in the San Francisco Bay Area, are now provided by one regionalized center. Other major personnel consolidations have taken place in the United Kingdom, Italy, and HP's European multi-country region. HP's Australasia location, which

TABLE 5

Advantages and Disadvantages to a Shared Services Delivery Approach

Advantages	Disadvantages
• Decreased cost	• Feelings of depersonalized service
• Increased efficiency	• Emergence of shadow staffs
• Increased productivity	• Costs to set up shared service centers
• Duplication and overlapping work can be eliminated	• Require a significant investment in automation technology
• Greater flexibility to meet customer needs	• Organizational resistance to losing on-site support

includes Australia and New Zealand, has gone to one personnel function for both sites, instead of having two. Disability claims management has been consolidated into a single disability service center to service all of HP's U.S. operations. Eventually, benefits administration and relocations, may be centralized at the corporate level.

The literature review and NAPA's interviews in the public and private sectors identified advantages and disadvantages to the shared services delivery approach which are presented in Table 5.

Advisory and Consultative Activities

Organizational entities need access to HR resources that can provide advice and assistance to resolve business-specific issues — the second "bucket" of HR activities. These HR professionals serve as advisors and consultants to managers to help implement business strategies and goals. They bring to the table technical HR expertise and change strategies that will help a business unit achieve desired results. They also have the expert HR knowledge to access the necessary resources needed to develop new programs and processes.

Aligning HR Advisory and Consultative Services with the Business Unit

One model for delivering these types of HR services is to align HR advisory and consultative resources directly with the business units. Hewlett-Packard, for example, has established management support teams to work with local management. These personnel generalists are located in the company's operating units and directly link HR to those units' business strategies. By maintaining on-site personnel professionals who can consult with managers on business-specific issues, HR can be more involved in correlating personnel knowledge and practices with business challenges.

Air Products' HR operations have evolved along a similar line. It began shifting HR people to the business units 10-15 years ago, starting with placing an HR director in the major business units to consult with the business unit head. Gradually they added staff and competencies in business units. The process was an evolutionary one, with more and more HR functions decentralized to the business units. It left centralized only

Structuring the Organization to Provide HRM Services

those functions it thought logically should be centralized, which include university recruiting, equal employment administration, compensation and benefits, training, and organization development.

The main advantage to this alignment of HR resources is that it helps the HR staff stay in touch with the needs of the business and create solutions that are business relevant and avoids "creating solutions looking for a strategy." A disadvantage is the amount of resources required to provide these services to all business units.

Reporting Relationship of HR Advisors and Consultants

Even though they work for the business unit, these HR specialists need a functional tie to the corporate HR department. In HP, the personnel generalists aligned with HP's business units report directly to the line managers of those units, but also have a dotted-line relationship with the vice president for personnel. Air Products' HR directors and staff in the business units also have a dotted-line reporting relationship into corporate HR. At Intel, the HR staff working on-site with the business units report to the corporate HR function and have a dotted-line relationship with site managers.

Centers of Excellence Providing Advisory and Consultative Services

Another model for providing these non-routine, and non-administrative, business consultant-type HR activities is the shared services environment. Individuals with extensive knowledge and expertise in organizational design and development, communication and other HR specialties are combined to work for Centers of Excellence rather than individual units. The organization's business units use these shared resources to solve problems. As customer needs are identified, these centers form teams of experts that can address the issues. While departments and agencies may prefer to have these business-related services provided by on-site HR professionals, small agencies or those with many small, widely-separated units may require a shared services alternative to provide a fuller range of options to clients.

One option within the Centers of Excellence approach is for business units to retain an HR business representative, or account manager, on-site to serve as the customer interface. This individual helps formulate the business unit's needs and translates HR initiatives into business results. S/he reports to the head of the business unit and is the dominant interface between shared services and business requirements. Their job is not always to do the work, but to facilitate the work effort being done by shared services. If they are doing their job well, they will minimize the growth of HR shadow staffs in the business units.

Advantages and Disadvantages to Centers of Excellence

Centers of Excellence have advantages and disadvantages similar to those listed for service centers (see Table 5). An additional difficulty may be the inability of a single HR entity to deal with multiple organizational missions and emphases embodied in the Center's customers. HR staff may find it difficult to truly understand a variety of missions and be flexible to tailor their advice to a variety of customers who may have different organizational priorities and values.

HR staff may find it difficult to truly understand a variety of missions and be flexible to tailor their advice to a variety of customers who may have different organizational priorities and values.

HR as a Strategic Partner

Several of the organizations NAPA interviewed view the strategic partner role to be that of consultant and advisor. Certainly, HR professionals who are strategic partners with management are often acting as consultants, advisors and change agents. Nevertheless, we have left this as a separate functional category (the third "bucket") because the focus of these activities transcends HR's relationship to problems at the business unit. Operating on the strategic level, HR can have an impact on the future direction and mission of an organization by ensuring that strategies consider the people impacts of business changes and initiatives.

The panel does not believe that a shared service delivery model is appropriate for the strategic partner activities. HR strategic partners ideally should be on-site; aligned with the top management team at the corporate and business unit level and dedicated to those business units.

Several factors may preclude an organization from assigning HR strategic resources to all major organizational units. Small agencies, in particular, may not have the resources to do so. In that case, a shared delivery services approach may be the only alternative to providing these services. In such a case, the HR organization should identify an individual or a team to be the primary contact point for business units for strategic HR advice.

Line Managers in the Service Delivery Model

As line managers are being held increasingly accountable for managing people they are being called upon to directly deliver HR services. Line managers deliver training programs and lead organizational change efforts. Air Products currently has a pilot underway that will enable line managers to use an automated systems module to view and execute pay changes and awards for their organizations.

Technology as a Service Delivery Mechanism

Improved technology, such as touch-tone phone systems and kiosks, is allowing a greater number of HR services to be performed by the customer. In addition to routine administrative processes, HR information technology has expanded to include more complex tasks, such as succession planning software, and modeling software which will enable an organization to project the effects of downsizing efforts. These technological improvements will enable HR professionals and line managers to better deliver necessary HR services and give HR professionals more time to devote to more value-added HR activities.

Traditional Service Delivery Model

In the traditional service delivery model, the majority of HR work is performed by HR professionals dedicated to the business units. This model is found throughout the federal government. Within a department, each bureau has its own full-service HR office as do many of the regional and/or district offices. This sometimes results in an agency having multiple HR offices in the same city. As processes are streamlined and technology finds ways to do work without face-to-face contact, this delivery mechanism is becoming less prominent.

Structuring the Organization to Provide HRM Services

Technological improvements will enable HR professionals and line managers to better deliver necessary HR services and give HR professionals more time to devote to more value-added HR activities.

A WORD ABOUT REENGINEERING

There is an abundant supply of sources of information on reengineering in books, journals, and training courses. While this report does not specify a preferred methodology, the following general suggestions are offered.

- Identify all HR processes which are performed.
- Determine candidates for reengineering based on criteria such as:
  - Importance to mission success
  - Value to the customer
  - Costs
  - Probability of success
- Involve all stakeholders, including providers and customers of the process, to decide what processes to reengineer.
- Once processes for reengineering are identified:
  - Obtain top management approval
  - Thoroughly train all participants in reengineering tools and techniques and change management strategies
  - Map processes to be reengineered
  - Ruthlessly eliminate non-value added steps
  - Assess opportunities to use information technology — determine costs and benefits
  - Develop new processes — with stakeholders' involvement
  - Develop change management strategy and roll-out plan
  - Communicate, Communicate, Communicate
  - Implement
  - Evaluate results
  - Continuously improve

The implications for agencies as they develop HR service delivery models are:

- HR's customers should help HR determine which HR practices and activities should be performed or discarded.
- Practices and activities that are not valued by HR's customers should be eliminated if not required by laws or regulations.
- Key HR processes should be reengineered and automated.
- Even if an organization does not have the time/resources to reengineer its HR function, it should realign HR activities to provide more coherent planning and service delivery. This can be done by combining HR's many specialty areas into a few functional clusters along the lines suggested in this chapter. The use of HR generalists for service delivery is a promising trend. This trend will contribute to simpler and more effective support to line managers and employees.

- Departments and agencies should develop criteria for how work should be performed — contracted out, franchised, or done internally — and then use the criteria to complete a rigorous review to determine the best service delivery method.
- For routine activities to be performed in-house, departments and agencies should consider shared services to achieve more efficient service delivery. Small agencies, in particular, should consider using shared services to better utilize limited resources.
- Strategic HR resources should be provided at the corporate (departmental) and business unit (bureau) levels if at all possible.

CHAPTER 5

Measurement

WHY MEASURE?

The notion that HR cannot be measured is sometimes given as a reason why managers are reluctant to invest more resources in people programs. Measurement is important to any operation, and is certainly key to reinventing human resources.

> "By definition, what gets measured is what is valued."
> Jac Fitz-enz

> Cramer's Law
> "Anything you measure improves."
> Quinn Cramer
> Hewlett-Packard

> "Individuals can perform at their best only if they are regularly, formally, and objectively measured. That process is the essence of accountability."
> Richard S. Sloma

EFFECTIVENESS AND EFFICIENCY

Measuring human resources activities and outcomes requires careful thought about the nature of the HR business. Just as the case for positive results from measurement is strong, measuring the wrong things can be self-defeating. Human resources' outputs are knowledge, ideas, and information. Usually another knowledge worker takes the HR output and uses it to produce something else. It is thus critical that HR work on the right

Human resources' outputs are knowledge, ideas, and information.

Measurement

However, becoming overly focused on efficiency measures can detract from effectiveness.

things because knowledge, ideas and information only have value if another person uses them to produce a product or service that is useful to the ultimate customer. First and foremost, HR measurement should focus on effectiveness, because HRM's contribution to organizational results is the most significant measure of its effectiveness.

Efficiency is also important and must be measured. This is especially true in public institutions that operate on tax dollars. However, becoming overly focused on efficiency measures can detract from effectiveness. NAPA found that some of the successful private firms we visited were more concerned with making sure their human resources management processes were effective than with whether they were the most efficient — as measured by costs and servicing ratios. In fact, HR servicing ratios in the 1:50 to 1:75 range were found in leading firms. These ratios are well above the 1:100 ratio sought by many federal agencies. Some firms dealt with being effective first, and then started to drive down costs and become more efficient as new policies and technology were brought on-line.

The approach the NPR took was to declare the HR system very ineffective, and then to implement major efficiency initiatives which will reduce the resource levels in HR by up to 50 percent. The NPR does not acknowledge the possibility of a positive return-on-investment by preserving more resources to make HR processes more effective. However, agencies would be well advised to devote resources to reengineer HR processes. Absent that, reduced HR staffs will be less capable of producing the current level of services and will not have the capability to perform more value-added activities.

FIGURE 6

What to Measure?

Organizational Success

- Is the organization achieving its goals in terms of productivity, quality, and customer service?
- What is the relationship of the human component of the organization to the success or failure of the organization in meeting its goals?
- How can the human component make a greater contribution to mission through actions taken by line managers and HR staff members?

Measurements

- Results of mission reviews and evaluation activities.
- Employee surveys to define satisfaction and beliefs re: barriers to performance.
- Surveys of satisfaction with HR services.
- HR Process Performance including key process cycle time, accuracy, and rework rates.

RESISTANCE TO MEASUREMENT

There are some on-going efforts to measure human resources. For example, the Saratoga Institute has established a measurement program that provides data to benchmark HR performance. OPM and the Equal Employment Opportunity Commission (EEOC) publish some information on workforce demographics, but there is limited information that measures effectiveness and efficiency of federal-wide HR operations. That which does exist tends to be gross information such as overall servicing ratios.

Why has a measurement system not been established? The NPR estimates that 40,000 people are engaged in human resources work—and this does not even account for the significant amount of time managers spend on HR duties. Fitz-enz (Human Value Management) offered insight into the resistance to measurement based on his experience in implementing HR measurement systems for the private sector. He identifies the following causes of resistance to measurement: (1) Habit: While some federal HR operations have systematically measured program inputs and outputs, most have not had a clear focus on results. (2) Fear: Perhaps there is a lack of information about the positive uses of measurement data to improve anything. If data are used primarily in a punitive manner, such as staff reduction, it is unlikely that HR will willingly adopt improved measurement. (3) Disagreement: There are people who believe HR should not be measured because it exists on a higher level than other work. How do you measure conscience? (4) Lack of Knowledge: Some HR staff do not understand how measurement can be used to help them and the organization be more successful.

If HR is to achieve the role as a full member of the leadership team, it is important that agency HR leaders ensure that a robust measurement system is in place and used as a management tool to improve operations.

WHAT TO MEASURE?

Measuring the right things is important for the reasons cited previously. Most important is measuring HR's contribution to organizational results.

Agencies regularly review how well they are accomplishing mission results. This will become even more prevalent as GPRA strategic plans and evaluations are introduced and perfected. HR managers must participate in these activities and identify ways to increase human contributions.

Understanding employee perceptions about the effectiveness and fairness of management practices is useful to managers and HR staffs as they work together to improve employee commitment and shared values. Comparative survey data

FIGURE 6, continued

What to Measure?

Efficiency

- What are labor costs including average salaries and average grade, sick leave usage, injury compensation costs?
- How much is it costing to accomplish HRM activities?
- What is the cost for various HR sub-functional activities such as recruitment, training, benefits administration, etc.?
- How do our costs compare with other HR organizations in our sector?
- What is the level of effort expended by managers and employees in order to use the HR processes which are essential to their jobs?
- What costs savings have been achieved due to employee suggestions and process improvements?

Measurements

- Average salary and grade, sick leave usage rates, and injury compensations costs.
- Servicing ratios for each sub-function.
- Costs per employee serviced for each sub-function.
- Comparative costs and ratios with other like organizations.
- Process mapping to level of effort for managers and employees in various key HR processes.
- Savings due to suggestion programs and other employee improvement initiatives.

Most important is measuring HR's contribution to organizational results.

Measurement

across the organization will provide a basis to address specific problems of management practices and communication deficiencies. Structured interviews can achieve improved understanding by asking managers: What is the problem and what are the probable causes? Why is it a problem? How will we know when the problem is solved?

Finally, HR can track its own effectiveness against established performance measures for cycle time, accuracy of information, and rework rates.

Controlling costs is always an important consideration in managing the federal workforce. It is important that the HR office be an active participant in this process, along with the financial management organization and line managers. Controlling costs requires a review of internal and comparative external costs. Done in conjunction with the analysis of organizational success, results of these reviews will provide useful insights into how to improve HR's contribution to organizational success and costs control.

Efficiency data should be assessed to determine costs trends. If benchmarking information is available, it should be used to determine if costs are unusual as compared with other like organizations. Understanding cost drivers for delivering HRM services provides valuable insights into opportunities for alternative sources of delivery (contracting).

It is valuable to also capture data which reflects cost savings due to employee suggestions or improvements in processes. HR can also show the benefits of its activities in this manner. For example, special emphasis programs to reduce sick leave usage or injury compensation costs can be established.

Trend data are invaluable for line managers and human resources specialists. These data establish a baseline and then serve as indicators that something in the workforce requires further examination. While the data normally will not provide the cause, they will provide valuable clues as to where to look for answers.

Benchmarking trend information will permit comparisons with other like

If benchmarking information is available, it should be used to determine if costs are unusual as compared with other like organizations.

FIGURE 6, continued

What to Measure?

Trend Data
- What are the major demographic trends within the workforce?
- What is the workload volume in various HR program areas?
- What are the indicators of workforce morale telling us?
- Are goals being accomplished in terms of diversity, staffing levels, workforce training, etc.?
- How does our trend data compare with other like organizations? What are plausible causes for variations?

Measurements
- Average age/retirement eligibility
- Average years in grade/promotion rate
- Racial and Ethnic Demographics
- Volume of actions processed in various HR subfunctions (staffing, classification/pay, training, employee relations, labor relations)
- Morale indicators such as grievance/complaints, appeals, law suits, sick leave usage, Employee Assistance Program usage, congressional inquiries, and voluntary attrition.
- Hiring and promotion rates for various age, racial and ethnic groups.
- Unfair labor practice charges, arbitrations, and other disputes with employee unions?

organizations and help determine whether solutions to emerging problems should be organization-specific or system wide. Trend data can also be used to forecast future events and plan actions to respond to projected prolems. The ability to anticipate problems enables managers and HR staffs to avoid crisis management.

Proactive analysis of trends will often demonstrate to senior management that HR has the business acumen to function as a member of the senior management team where analysis of program performance is a valued commodity.

The following actions will enhance agencies' abilities to use measurement as a tool to improve HR's ability to contribute to organizational mission, people and efficiency goals:

- Establish reporting and evaluation processes to ensure that HRM measurement captures information that is most important to agency mission results. Involve line managers in the process. The scope of this activity should include considering the human component of mission results included in GPRA strategic plans.
- Measure employee satisfaction on a regular basis. This information should be used to hold managers and HR staff accountable for effective HRM.
- Conduct regular surveys and structured interviews to assess satisfaction with HR services. This information is a key accountability tool to assess HR performance effectiveness, and to identify needed improvement initiatives.
- Train HR staffs in data analysis and statistical techniques so that they can evaluate program results and trends as a basis for improving HR operations.
- OPM should establish, or facilitate creation of, benchmarks for HR efficiency. The measures should be specific enough to allow for valid comparisons with like operations.

OPM should establish, or facilitate creation of, benchmarks for HR efficiency.

CHAPTER 6

Achieving More Effective Human Resources Management: A Strategy

Many leading private firms and innovative public sector organizations, as described in the NAPA literature review and innovative practices compendium, clearly demonstrate the value of effective HRM. Properly defined, organized, led, resourced, and trained, the HRM component of an organization becomes a major value-adding element that contributes to the achievement of organizational goals and business results. The value-added model for HRM is defined by the general characteristics shown in Figure 7.

This model varies considerably from the typical federal model in several important respects. The characteristics of the current system have been discussed in detail in various reports (NAPA 1983, MSPB 1993, and NPR 1994), and are summarized in the literature review that accompanies this report. These reports cited a system that was centrally-controlled, stifled innovation, prevented tailoring programs to mission, expensive, and ineffective. The challenge is how to move to a model that enables HRM processes to make a positive difference to organizational performance. To date there has been an inadequate movement toward increased agency discretion to develop HR organizations and policies which are responsive to their missions. Meanwhile, major reductions are being made in HR staffing levels, without benefit of legislative changes that would increase efficiency by empowering of managers and employees to perform more HR functions. The time for action is now!

The challenge is how to move to a model that enables HRM processes to make a positive difference to organizational performance.

ACHIEVING A NEW MODEL

The following actions are fundamental to changing the longstanding federal HRM reputation as a barrier to effective operation of government programs.

Stating a Clear Vision: Agency leaders and Congress must be clear about the value and role of effective HRM in federal government operations. They must clearly state expectations for an HRM system driven by mission results and linked in a visible way to agency strategy, as described in GPRA. The role and expectations for agency managers and HR directors should be contained in legislation, similar to the statute that established the chief financial officers. As part of the legislation, agencies should be given authority to develop their own human resources systems, tailored to their cultures, missions, and the labor market norms for their occupations.

Achieving More Effective Human Resources Management: A Strategy

Agency leaders and Congress must be clear about the value and role of effective HRM in federal government operations.

FIGURE 7

Value-Added Model for HRM

- Line management is in charge of, and accountable for, HR processes. There is a general recognition of the vital role of the human component plays in meeting organizational goals. Line managers are well trained in effective HRM practices and techniques.
- HR is measured by the value it adds to the organization's mission accomplishment.
- HR is a respected part of the organization's leadership. Often reporting to the top executive, but always having regular and ready access to the senior manager.
- HR staffing, organization, technology strategy, policies and practices are developed based on the results being sought by the organization, rather than concepts from other sources. Shared services are used where they contribute to efficiency without loss of core mission capability.
- Corporate offices (departments) give business units (bureaus) considerable latitude to tailor their HR programs within the construct of very general policies and principles. The corporate HR staff is valued for its ability to facilitate business unit results and support corporate strategic planning.
- HR staffs and managers develop HR competencies which enable them to apply HR principles to solve business problems. HR functional knowledge is a means — not an end.
- HR staffs have broad business skills which augment a high level of expertise in the basics of human resources management. Hiring and developing HR staff focuses on the ability to apply HR competence to improve organizational performance and goal attainment.

Centrally-controlled processes should be limited to those that are not core to missions. Core HRM processes include: hiring; compensating; training; motivating; and leading. Eliminating the Federal Personnel Manual is a positive step in that direction. But more fundamental change is needed.

Accountability should be clearly stated in terms of developing and utilizing human resources effectively to meet current mission and future strategic goals and should be reflected in the agency's performance management system. Accountability includes operating within the context of legal boundaries, such as those contained in EEO, Fair Labor Standards Act (FLSA), Occupational Safety and Health Administration (OSHA) statutes, and merit principles. The current approach to merit should be revised to be more flexible and emphasize competence rather than processes that create barriers to managers trying to meet their legitimate hiring needs. Accountability for results will be easier to establish once Congress grants agencies flexibility to tailor HR systems and the human component contributing to mission results is included in GPRA s strategic plans.

Continuity of Leadership: The administration and Congress must address the problems caused by frequent turnover of political appointees who manage the civil service. Average tenure is approximately 18 months. A new approach that ensures responsiveness to policy directions sought by elected officials while providing for continuity and professional expertise will contribute to improved government performance and better management of the civil service. While many approaches are possible, NAPA sug-

TABLE 6

HR Training needs for Line Managers

Manager-Identified Line Management Training Needs	Employee-Identified Line Management Training Needs
• Personnel System Operation • Teamwork Processes • Business Management Skills • Problem-solving Techniques • Communication Techniques • Leadership/Motivation	• Personnel System Operation • People Skills • Ability to Deal with Change • Leadership Skills • Supervisory Skills • Communication Techniques

gests that the model now being used by New Zealand, which includes renewable time-limited appointments and performance contracts for senior operating executives, be considered as an alternative.

Building Line Management's Human Resources Competence: A general concern was expressed during focus group discussions about the competence of federal managers to assume a greater HRM role. Employees and line managers identified a number of skill deficits to address, as shown in Table 6.

HR specialists also noted areas related to management performance that need to be addressed in order to move to a decentralized model where managers performed more of their own HRM responsibilities. These include:

- Managers need to thoroughly learn the personnel system and develop strong people skills.
- Managers need to improve their problem-solving skills.
- Managers need to be held accountable for the HRM outcomes that result from their actions.

Agencies must undertake a focused effort to identify and provide training on the critical competencies managers need to operate in a human resources system where there are fewer rules, tailored agency systems, expanded delegation of authority and line management accountability for results. Two critical competencies for line managers are supervisory skills and leadership skills. A conceptual model of training programs in these two areas is shown in Table 7.

Professionalization of Human Resources Staff: As discussed in the literature review, human resources staffs need to improve their professional reputation and competence to gain acceptance as a strategic partner. A major effort such as that undertaken by AT&T to professionalize its HR staff (see the compendium of innovative practices) will

Managers need to thoroughly learn the personnel system and develop strong people skills.

be needed to build the capability essential to move from the current state to one like that described in the value-added HR model presented earlier. During focus groups, managers, employees and HR specialists were asked to identify what additional skills and competencies were needed by HR staffs needed in order to improve their performance. A partial summary is shown in Table 8.

A review o.f the innovative practices compendium yielded a similar list of HR competency requirements, including:

- Know the Business
- Computer Systems
- Strategic Thinking
- Leadership Models
- Team Skills
- Communication Skills
- Continuous Learning
- Know How HR Applies in Mission
- Change Management
- TQM and Reengineering
- Quantitative Analysis
- Interpersonal Relations Skills
- Service Delivery Concepts
- Managing Contractors/Consultants

TABLE 7

A Supervisory and Leadership Skills Training Model

Supervisory Skills	Leadership Skills
- Supervisory role	- Creating a vision/mission statement
- Financial management	- Serving as a role model
- Safety & health programs	- Setting challenging goals
- EEO & diversity	- Measuring results
- Supply & logistics/facilities	- Representing the organization
- Staffing	- Encouraging employee participation
- Organizing work & classification	- Fostering team work
- Motivation & incentives	- Solving problems & making decisions
- Labor-management relations	- Using diversity to improve decisions
- Performance management	- Establishing fact-based analysis/decisions
- Training & development	- Maintaining knowledge of external and internal environment
- Discipline & adverse actions	- Coaching employees and teams
- Employee conduct/ethics	- Delegating & maintaining accountability
- Communications/providing feedback	- Managing change
	- Mentoring

TABLE 8

Skills and Competencies Needed by HR Staffs

Employees	Managers	HR Specialists
• Consulting Skills • Generalist HR Knowledge • Line Management Orientation • Analytical Skills • Team Process Skills • Customer Focus • Planning Skills • ADP Knowledge • Flexibility • Innovation	• Mission Knowledge • ADP Knowledge • Communication Skills • Change Management Skills • Business Skills • Risk Taking • Generalist HR Knowledge • Team Process Skills • Work Planning & Prioritization Skills • People Skills	• HR Knowledge • Communication Skills • Problem Solving Skills • Time Management Skills • ADP Knowledge • TQM Skills • Consulting Skills • Systems Approach • Innovation

Putting these competencies in the context of the Ulrich model discussed in the literature review yields a useful model for considering HR staff development.

At present, there is no source of training that adequately addresses these issues in the context of federal HRM concepts and practices. Most of these topics can be found in courses taught by universities, private organizations, and professional societies, but without the federal context.

There needs to be a concentrated effort by agencies to identify a curriculum of HR courses to use to guide the development of HR staff and leaders to function in the various roles described in this report. The information contained in this report, along with the accompanying literature review and compendium of innovative practices can be used as a starting point for this effort.

There also needs to be a method for ensuring that HR staffs, especially at the higher levels, possess a high level understanding of HRM and management practices. This can be achieved via a professional certification program (see the literature review for detail).

Finally, HR leaders need to consider the process for filling future HR vacancies. Individuals with advanced degrees in business administration or an HR specialty are considered top candidates in many of the organizations NAPA interviewed. Also considered desirable are people who can bring practical business knowledge to the job. HR staff hiring practices are discussed in more detail in the literature review.

Functioning as a strategic partner and change agent entails a different set of competencies, which are generally obtainable only through post high school education. Successful performance of administrative functions does not prepare employees to serve in these more demanding roles. Changing the policy will likely cause concern among the secretarial and administrative staff who have achieved their upward mobility goals via a position in personnel or human resources. A possible solution is to provide encouragement, through tuition assistance, for those individuals who are motivated to seek positions in human resources to obtain the appropriate academic

FIGURE 8

A Model for HR Staff Development	
Strategic Partner - Know the mission, customers, services - Be able to find solutions to business problems - Know business processes: finance, MIS, control systems, measurement & accountability - Understand human behavior & team processes - Know organization design principles - Be able to effectively consult with senior management - Exhibit self confidence & action orientation - Communicate well in all situations	**Change Agent** - Knowledge of change process - Consultation skills - Ability to build trust with clients - Listening skills - Communications with all levels - Ability to influence others to take action - Ability to work in teams - Knowledge of measurement and analysis - Knowledge of human behavior - Problem solving - Quantitative analyses - TQM/Reengineering
Administrative Expert - Knowledge of HR laws and policies - Ability to apply HR program knowledge including: recruitment, selection, & placement; classification and compensation; benefits; labor-management relations; employee relations; health & safety; security to meet business needs - Applied knowledge of customer service - Knowledge of TQM, reengineering, and use of information technology to improve efficiency and service. - Action orientation	**Employee Champion** - Knowledge of line and staff roles - Ability to design & conduct surveys - Knowledge of motivation theory - Skill in dispute resolution - Knowledge of measurement and analysis - Skill in creating participative environment - Knowledge of HR legal and policy framework - Listening skills - Ability to influence others to take action

background to be fully equipped to serve in the multiple roles now expected of leading-edge HR operations. Where bargaining unit employees may be affected, agencies should consider addressing this issue in their labor-management partnerships forums.

Coping with HR Staff Reductions: Reductions in HR staff at a greater rate than the general reductions in federal government employment are inevitable. This is due in no small part to many years of criticisms about inflexible, unresponsive, and ineffective HR systems that agencies had little role in developing and for which they accepted little ownership. As a result, HR staffs may find they are unable to continue providing the same level of service, let alone take on some of the new roles described in this report.

The preferred approach would have been to address effectiveness issues first, and then achieve increased efficiency. However, agencies and private sector employers have actions underway to cope with reduced HR staffing which can serve as a guide to federal agencies faced with staff reductions. Many of these strategies are discussed in the accompanying literature review and compendium of innovative practices. In addition, material provided in this report (Chapter 3 — Management/employee self-sufficiency and the use of technology; Chapter 5 — Using measurement systems to manage and focus HR activities; Chapter 4 — Process improvement and reengineering and alternative options for service delivery) provide a range of approaches agencies can use to operate HR more effectively with fewer resources. These approaches must necessarily be augmented by substantial quantities of vision, persistence, skill, persuasiveness, energy and will power.

Special Needs of Small Agencies: As described at Appendix C to this report, small agencies have some special needs due to resources limitations. Many smaller agencies do not have a dedicated policy and program staff to undertake broad developmental activities associated with major changes in HRM statutes or polices. It is difficult for small agencies to develop unique tailored solutions. Given the probability of a major paradigm shift in federal HRM programs, it may be advantageous for small agencies to consider opportunities to franchise out those operational aspects of HRM that can be provided by other sources. This can be achieved while maintaining the capability to serve as a strategic partner and provide consultative services to their line managers. Contracting or franchising major HR information technology operations and development is one area where small agencies can enjoy the benefits of economies of scale by partnering with large agencies. Other areas which should be examined for outsourcing or franchising include staffing, training, benefits administration, and records maintenance.

Actions suggested to improve the performance the federal HRM system are:
- Congress should address problems associated with the frequent turnover of, and qualification requirements for, political leaders responsible for managing civil servants involved in operational functions.
- Develop training programs — for managers, employees and HR specialists — designed to improve performance of the HRM system at all levels. A recommended conceptual model for such a program is provided in Table 7 and Figure 8.
- The federal HR community should develop an HR professional certification program to ensure a high quality HR staff throughout the government. In the initial years, certification should be used as a training needs identification tool. In

As a strategy for dealing with HR staff reductions, invest in technology to provide the infrastructure to empower employees and managers to perform more of their own HR work.

future years it should be used as a requirement for promotion to senior HR positions at grades GS-13 and above.

- As a strategy for dealing with HR staff reductions, invest in technology to provide the infrastructure to empower employees and managers to perform more of their own HR work. In addition, agencies should continue to aggressively pursue opportunities to collaborate on system improvements such as the current project to develop "Employee Express."
- Small agencies should consider opportunities to contract out HR operational functions to other providers while retaining the ability to perform the strategic advisor role for their agency.

APPENDIX A

Literature Review Summary

The National Academy of Public Administration (NAPA) federal agencies to respond to the National Performance Review (NPR) and other forces which demand major changes in human resources management (HRM).

The literature analysis part of this project includes a review of literature, journal articles, publications, and books by leading HRM practitioners and theorists regarding issues and concepts relating to HRM roles, structures, service delivery systems, and competencies. A total of 367 references were reviewed. A complete bibliography starts on page 66.

The literature review was guided by the following research questions:
- What are the roles of major participants and stakeholders in the HRM process?
- What is the scope of HRM functions and activities?
- What are the expectations regarding HRM's contribution to organizational performance and other values such as equity and fairness? What are the current and desired levels of performance?
- What are the characteristics of effective HRM?
- What are the key issues affecting human resources (HR) organization and staffing.
- What are the skill/competency requirements necessary for HR professionals to successfully accomplish their roles?
- What is the current status of civil service reform at all levels of government?
- What lessons can be learned from current and past civil service reform efforts? How does the approach to the NPR compare with these efforts?
- What are the key elements of HRM's capacity to perform desired roles?
- What does the literature say about accountability for HRM in decentralized public organizations?

An organization needs HRM to make it a place where people can achieve their personal goals while at the same time helping the institution accomplish its mission.

Literature Review Summary

PURPOSE OF HRM

The fundamental consideration in determining the roles, responsibilities, and organization for HRM responsibilities is the purpose to be achieved. Jac Fitz-enz speaks to this issue by noting that an organization needs HRM "to make it a place where people can achieve their personal goals while at the same time helping the institution accomplish its mission."[1] Fitz-enz goes on to state that this approach differs from the common notion of HRM which focuses on program administration. Rather, HRM needs to direct attention to adding value by helping the organization achieve its production, financial, and human objectives. He further comments that this approach to human resources will benefit the organization, and reposition HRM within the organization from an administrative function to a strategic partner.[2]

Firms using more progressive human resources policies generally had superior financial performance.

There is increasing empirical support for the importance of HR practices to organizational performance. In a recent study, Mark Huselid of Rutgers University, examined work practices and financial performance in over 700 publicly held firms.[3] The study examined best practices in the areas of: personnel selection, job design, information sharing, performance appraisal, promotion systems, attitude assessment, incentive systems, grievance procedures, and labor management participation. Huselid found that firms using more progressive human resources policies generally had superior financial performance. For example, annual stockholder return for the top 25 percent of the progressive practice firms was 9.4 percent versus 6.5 percent for the bottom 25 percent. Gross return on capital was 11.3 percent for the top 25 percent versus 3.5 percent for the bottom 25 percent of the firms. After accounting for other factors likely to influence financial performance (such as industry characteristics), the HR index remained related significantly to both performance measures. This same index was also associated with higher sales per worker, lower employee turnover, and improved price-cost margin (gross profits before depreciation/net sales).

Another study of HRM and economic performance examined 150 of the Forbes 500 firms.[4] HR practices were grouped into six main areas: participation and management style, culture, organizational structure, creativity, reward systems, and flexibility and accommodation of needs. A "progressivity" index was created using these areas. The 75 most progressive and 75 least progressive firms were identified. The annual change in performance of these firms was then compared over a six-year period. The results are:

Annual Change in Financial Performance: 1978-83

Measure	75 Most Progressive	75 Least Progressive
Profit growth	10.8%	2.6%
Sales growth	17.5%	10.7%
Growth in Earnings per Share	6.2%	(-3.9%)
Dividend Income	13.4%	9.2%

Ulrich and Yeung describe the importance of the HR program to the success of organizations as follows: "HR has a key role to play in developing a competitive advantage by attracting the best people, and instituting organizational systems and processes that enable individuals to add value within the larger organizational unit."[5] They cite three reasons why HR should play a central role in creating and sustaining a competitive advantage. First, people cause strategies to happen. Second, HR practices, such as compensation, performance management, and promotion processes, help to establish and reinforce a shared mind-set and shape behavior within organizations. Finally, HR builds capacity for change, which enables organizations to adapt to their environment. In conclusion, contemporary literature supports the premise that the human element is a vital factor in the successful performance of organizations.

CHARACTERISTICS OF EFFECTIVE HRM

The NPR accompanying report on human resources calls for a system, "in which the President, Congress and through them, citizens will hold agency managers accountable for mission accomplishment while adhering to principles of merit, equity and equal opportunity." The system would be characterized by decentralization, deregulation, simplicity, flexibility, and substantially increased delegations of authority. Key dimensions of this system include:

- Management ownership and accountability for HRM.
- HRM staffs which serve as advisors and are viewed as part of the management team. The success of their support is measured by contributions to achieving the agency's mission, goals and priorities.
- Agencies are permitted to tailor their HRM programs to meet unique needs as they arise, consistent with the fundamental principles of merit and equity and the government-wide legal framework. Mistakes or failures to comply with regulations should not prompt more stringent regulations. Instead individual violators should be held accountable for their actions.
- Authority to make HRM decisions is vested in line managers and delegated to the lowest practical level, including self-managed teams.
- Executives and managers value the federal workforce, and labor and management are partners in carrying out each agency's mission.[6]

Schay, while conducting research for the Office of Personnel Management (OPM), identified 10 criteria for effective HRM programs. They are:

- **Speed.** This item relates to cycle time for personnel actions such as hiring and classification.
- **Cost.** How much does it cost to deliver HR services? This includes "shadow" personnel positions which exist to perform functions managers desire that the personnel organization cannot, or will not, perform.
- **Quality.** Because quality is measured by the customer, one of the principal measures is customer satisfaction. In this study, low cost was negatively correlated with customer satisfaction. Successful results were achieved where total quality management (TQM) initiatives were in place to achieve process improvements and when personnel management advisors were assigned to line managers.
- **Flexible and Simple.** Successful operations had instituted one-stop shopping for personnel services, had shorter regulations, and more delegation to managers.

Measures are typically directed toward outputs and outcomes.

Literature Review Summary

- **Results versus Process Oriented.** A greater focus on measurement methods was apparent. Agency and HRM strategic planning initiatives were present. Measures were typically directed toward outputs and outcomes.

- **Empowered and Entrepreneurial.** Managers had considerable delegation to take personnel actions. Personnel offices were more likely to be engaged in cross-servicing arrangements.

- **Mission Driven.** HRM initiatives were related to agency missions through strategic plans and outcomes were measured.

- **Fair Treatment/Equal Opportunity.** This item was characterized by active recruitment programs with management involvement, emphasis on diversity, and the presence of labor-management partnerships and alternative dispute resolution techniques.

- **Productivity through People.** Personnel activities, such as training and family-friendly workplace, were viewed as investments. Activities designed to evaluate the state of HRM through such vehicles as employee surveys and organizational assessments were likely to be present.

- **Appropriate Centralization/Decentralization.** Standardized functions, i.e., benefits administration, were centralized to gain economies of scale. Unless there was value added by centralization, the functions were decentralized.[7]

Another perspective on the desired state of HR are the Saratoga Institute characteristics for effective HRM. According to Carter, the characteristics have nothing to do with the technical excellence of HR professionals, but rather relate to values and beliefs which motivate the best HR organizations to practice differently from the norm. These characteristics include:

- **Communications.** World-class HR organizations go to great lengths to communicate with the workforce and put significant effort into stimulating and supporting upward communications. Ingenuity in methods is found, but the key to best-practice HR functions' communications is the effort made to make communications a daily, primary duty of the entire staff.

- **Interdependence.** Best-practice HR functions realize that the work of one HR area affects the work of others. The territoriality of some HR groups is counterproductive. World-class HR functions, have on-going and regular formal and informal meetings across the subgroups to review the interdependent effects of one group's work on another.

- **Strategy and planning.** Best-practice HR departments actually work from a strategy and then prepare operating plans, specific objectives, and actions that lead the HR effort. Evidence and testimony suggest that this unusual capability stems from having a well-considered, clearly articulated, and thoroughly disseminated vision of the HR role within the enterprise. Strategy is defined broadly to include role, relationships, and contributions to corporate imperatives. A key success criteria is HR's involvement at the strategic level.

- **Commitment.** "Staying the course" is common TQM jargon for long-term commitment by top management. Best-practice HR departments are showcases of commitment to a vision of constant improvement. Not bound by methodology, these staffs develop programs and processes that lead to the vision, and the

The best-practice HR functions are proactive in their quest to go to their customers and ask what they are trying to achieve.

methodologies used depend on what vision needs to be realized. Flexibility, dynamism, and creativity are part of these HR cultures.

- **Customer-focused.** All HR departments claim to be customer-focused. All companies do, too. But the best-practice HR functions are proactive in their quest to go to their customers and ask what they are trying to achieve. This focus on the customers' objectives is the guiding light for assessing what types of HR problems or opportunities exist. Only in response to this feedback do the best-practice HR staffs return to the customer with recommendations that will assist them. Diagnosing customer needs as they relate to human issues is a way of life.

- **Never satisfied.** We often hear that customers are never satisfied and that, once a need is filled, there is always another need or want. That is what "the customer as a moving target" means. So, too, with best-practice HR departments. They are never satisfied. Even though the best-practice departments in the Saratoga Institute report were considered in the 95th percentile of over 500 HR functions studies, none of them were satisfied with their results! No matter what exceptional results were achieved, they had an idea or plan to make it better.

- **Risk taking.** Total reorganizations, restructuring job descriptions and titles, dropping services, and reallocating resources to more value-added products are examples of actions that best-practice HR groups have taken to become more efficient and effective. Although these types of actions are generally risky, world-class organizations are willing to experiment to be the best.

- **Culture consciousness.** Best-practice people believe that culture is critical in designing systems that will change behaviors. The process goes something like this: Culture drives systems, systems drive behavior, and behavior drives results. This is not meant to imply that cultures do not change. Rather, it implies that confluence with the culture is important, and the HR professional's role is to support some aspects of the culture as well as help change it when necessary.

- **Relationships.** Best-practice people described over and over how they had worked with key individuals to obtain their support. They acknowledged that all the technical HR knowledge in the world would not have made the difference without that support. The key to success was the relationship built and traded on when needed.[8]

The U.S. Merit Systems Protection Board (MSPB) concluded that the ideal role for personnel offices, based on comments from both managers and personnelists, included such factors as: being proactive; thinking like managers — considering themselves part of the management team; concentrating on the big picture rather than pushing paper; being mission and service oriented; and providing options to managers. To perform this role, personnelists responding to the MSPB survey wanted to be involved in management decisions at the front end (at the take-off as well as at the hard landing), to take a broad perspective of the organization, as well as to have the technical capabilities to advise managers, and to help managers with strategic planning for developing a representative workforce.[9]

The 1983 NAPA study envisioned a new conceptual framework for HRM which involved a more direct and active role for line managers. This would involve greater delegation of authority and increased involvement in the design of personnel systems and

Literature Review Summary

programs. The personnel staffs would establish consultative relationships with line managers to give professional guidance and assistance.

The goal would be to obtain, "... in fact focus more on providing direction, leadership, and evaluation. This would involve greater delegation to agencies to execute their personnel programs providing direction, leadership, and evaluation. This would involve greater delegation to agencies to execute their personnel programs."[10]

Fitz-enz calls for shifting the HR focus from programs to customers and from expense to value added. According to Fit-enz, the HR function must reexamine itself in the same way as a business needing a transformation. This includes vision, mission, and markets/customers. HR should ask what benefits it contributes to the organization in terms of human benefits (quality of work life), production benefits (helping employees become more efficient and achieve higher quality), and monetary benefits (contributing to the bottom line). These questions should be answered in terms of outcomes rather than inputs and processes (programs and procedures).[11]

The literature contains many examples of companies which have taken actions to make HRM more consistent with the characteristics of the desired state described above. For instance:

- Frito-Lay states the HR mission is to "create a team-oriented, owner-based and performance-driven culture that guarantees our company's industry leadership." HR stays aligned with Frito-Lay's business by establishing initiatives in such areas as internal governance, productivity improvement, customer service, and capacity building with HR through a competency model.
- Hewlett-Packard has defined the business of HR as facilitating, measuring, and improving the quality of the management process — as a complement to the management process, not a substitute for it. It has established a number of HRM initiatives which support their corporate strategic intent by increasing value, providing higher quality and utilizing resources more efficiently.
- Merck's HR mission is to enhance the corporate competitive advantage by enabling the company to attract, retain, develop and deploy its people to achieve optimal results. They have established initiatives to achieve this mission.[12]

ACCOUNTABILITY

The perception that there is a dichotomy between the manager's operations tasks and people tasks is not new. In 1948, McGregor wrote: "Members of line management tend to separate the management function into two distinct categories. On the one hand are the planning, the making of decisions and giving of orders. They are 'management.' They are 'getting out the production.' In the other category are the problems that arise and the work necessary to prevent such problems from arising (such as training supervisors, promoting employee cooperation). These to them are human relations, and not management."[13] While this perception is still evident in both the public and private sectors today, the literature speaks of a new operational role for line managers in the HRM arena, both here and around the world. The predominant theme running throughout the literature, for both public and private sector organizations, is increased decentralization and devolution of responsibility to line managers for managing human resources.

The predominant theme running throughout the literature, for both public and private sector organizations, is increased decentralization and devolution of responsibility to line managers for managing human resources.

A shift in responsibility for HRM from professional HR staff to line managers cannot take place without a corresponding shift in accountability. Because of its concern for waste, fraud and abuse, the American system has consistently chosen accountability over effective and efficient administration. The personnel system is no exception. Managers have been overburdened with rules and regulations that were originally designed to constrain partisan political influence in personnel matters. In recent decades, these limits have curbed managers' discretion as well.

Romzek and Dubnick conclude that reforms intended to increase managers' flexibility must address the accountability systems in the American public administration system. They postulate that accountability mechanisms in the United States vary along two dimensions: source of control and degree of control. The source of control relates to the origin or the expectation(s) (internal or external), and the relationship of the stakeholder(s) to the agency or individual. The degree of control can range from high to low.

Public personnel management systems are strategically focused on process. The emphasis is on the availability of procedures that can be activated, as necessary, to enforce rules and regulations. Romzek and Dubnick contend that more flexibility in the federal personnel system is needed to relieve the poor fit between the highly bureaucratized merit system and the needs of federal agencies and employees. The structures and processes of the public service system should be changed to shift the emphasis from negative controls and regulatory oversight as primary vehicles for accountability towards managerial discretion and professional responsibility. The public personnel system must also acknowledge its dependence on multiple accountability systems. Public employees face mandates with many facets. The expectations created should be matched with an appropriate accountability mechanism. For example, in order to take full advantage of Senior Executive Service (SES) members' expertise and experience, personnel practices related to them should be designed and managed in the context of professional and political accountability systems and not encumbered under a bureaucratic one.[14]

Companies that were successful in bringing about change, especially when HRM was used as a change agent, used organizational streamlining as a key feature. Using AT&T, the Bechtel Corporation, Delta Airlines and the State of California as models, the study concluded that managers must take greater control over critical personnel functions and become accountable for personnel management. Personnel management functions and routine personnel administration operations, such as selections, compensation (usually within limitations), training, development, promotions, and separations, were delegated to line managers so that they could retain control over those personnel activities which directly affect their respective organizational units. As line managers are more accountable for improved productivity, they need greater control over human resources, along with a corresponding balance of authority to allocate and reallocate human and material resources.[15]

The themes from this 1980's study are strongly reflected throughout the literature. The MSPB notes that managers have a key role to play in partnership with personnelists, in determining the quality of service they receive. To carry out their role effectively, managers need to have good supervisory skills and sufficient decision-making authority

Literature Review Summary

Managers will be trusted to act fairly and responsibly in managing their employees, and will be held accountable for their actions for achieving a productive, diverse, multi-skilled, customer-oriented workforce.

delegated to them. NAPA proposed a new conceptual framework in which "Federal executives and managers must take a more direct and active role in personnel... The Federal system must delegate more 'hands-on' authority to these managers and deliberately draw them more into the design of personnel systems and programs, so that the managerial needs will dominate design rather than procedural concerns."[16] "...NPR's recommendations for reinventing HRM call for maximum deregulation and delegation, trust, accountability for results, decentralization, and entrepreneurial behavior. Managers will be trusted to act fairly and responsibly in managing their employees, and will be held accountable for their actions for achieving a productive, diverse, multi-skilled, customer-oriented workforce."[17] The NPR recommendations attempt to recast the traditional personnel administration function into a progressive management function, and recognize that new practices and "deregulating" the personnel system by delegating more personnel authority to managers will not work unless it is done in concert with a wide integration of management functions.

Managers' Views of Accountability

Between mid-November 1991 and early February 1992, OPM distributed a Survey of Federal Employees to randomly-selected federal employees. Surveys were mailed to 57,000 employees; nearly 32,000 (56 percent) were returned. The results support the perception that federal managers do not have much authority in personnel matters. Nearly three-fourths of the respondents (73 percent) did not believe they had enough authority to determine their employees' pay. Slightly more than half (52 percent) did not believe they had enough authority to hire competent employees, and 49 percent did not believe they had enough authority to promote their employees. Only 25 percent maintained that they did not have enough authority to discipline poor performers.[18]

In 1991, the MSPB administered questionnaires to 72 personnelists and 269 managers in four federal agencies to examine federal managers' and personnelists' perceptions of personnel service delivery. MSPB found that "many managers were clearly reluctant to accept responsibility for personnel management." They viewed the system's procedures and regulations more as obstacles than aids to good management. When delegations had been made, they appeared to be in name only; managers believed that final decisions were still reserved for higher level management. While many supported a greater delegation of authority, others did not want the greater administrative burden they felt this would impose.[19]

While many supported a greater delegation of authority, others did not want the greater administrative burden they felt this would impose.

Thirty-two percent of the supervisory respondents to the MSPB survey indicated that they did not have the authority to initiate a personnel action. Only 52 percent had the authority to select employees and 36 percent had the authority to promote employees.[20] Given the state of training, perhaps limitations on authority are warranted, but the intent of the NPR to delegate authority to the lowest levels of management is surely a long way from reality based on this data.

Supervisory authority is critical to influencing employees to exhibit behaviors which are desired by the organization. Steer notes that supervisors can achieve employee commitment or compliance if they perceive that the supervisor has power. This power can be due to the supervisor's charisma, expertise, or position. But, it can also be reward power.[21] If supervisors lack authority to act in areas important to employees, they are lacking basic tools which are important to their success.

HR Functional Scope and Staffing

The literature describes traditional functions that HR staff perform, but also indicates that other roles are emerging. The activities and programs commonly assigned to HR are addressed in a report published by the Bureau of National Affairs, Inc. (BNA), which provides the survey results of 628 private companies.[22]

The survey addressed 55 HR activities and programs categorized under nine major functions. These include:
- Employment and recruiting
- Training and development
- Compensation
- Benefits
- Employee services
- Employee and community relations
- Personnel records
- Health and safety
- Strategic planning

The survey results show that activities performed by HR staff exclusively are most often those that involve compensation, benefits, and recruiting. Also, HR often shares responsibility for employee communications, training, and employment interviews with other departments. HR departments in 37 percent of responding firms took on new activities during the past year; just five percent gave up duties.[23]

The survey results also showed that companies with a larger workforce were more inclined to undertake certain activities than their counterparts with fewer than 1,000 employees. In addition, HR departments in larger establishments were more likely to handle all aspects of incentive pay, executive compensation, job analysis, and job evaluation than in smaller firms. On the other hand, while smaller employers tended to assign worker's compensation, wellness, employee communications, and community relations programs to HR alone, larger firms more frequently assigned these areas to other departments.[24]

Of special interest to the NAPA HRM project is that the HR departments in the surveyed organizations were rarely excluded from strategic planning activities. Strategic planning and decision making typically were shared with other departments. A majority of firms gave HR partial responsibility for handling organization development and mergers/acquisitions planning. Employers were more inclined to grant HR exclusive dominion over HR forecasting and international personnel administration.[25]

The HR department's authority frequently transcended "traditional" HR activities. Sixty-eight percent of the surveyed HR departments oversaw one or more general services or administrative support functions for their companies. Additions to HR department responsibilities fell primarily into administrative and general support activities. Many were in food services, security, child care, office/clerical support, risk management, or maintenance/facility management. Several HR departments took on TQM or

Literature Review Summary

Every HR system influences employee performance and thus, the success or failure of the total quality initiative.

Literature Review Summary

other quality improvement plans, safety programs, training and development, or payroll administration.[26]

HR's Role in Total Quality Management

One of HR's emerging roles is TQM planning and implementation. A number of recent publications have discussed the growing relationship between HR and total quality programs within organizations. Ulrich, speaking about the emerging role of HR in the total quality arena, says that the "unique and increasing HR involvement becomes less a missionary movement and more a management reality."[27] He goes on to say that the HR role is to help all employees develop a new mindset for a shared commitment to quality in everyday work. Roth supports this view, saying, "It should be obvious...that the human resources function is better equipped than any other to organize and facilitate a quality improvement process."[28]

Caudron states definitively that "...every HR system influences employee performance and thus, the success or failure of the total quality initiative."[29] She goes on to say that keeping HR systems aligned with quality strategies will be the HR challenge of the next decade. But, at the same time, this doesn't mean that HR should lead a quality effort. Caudron quotes Ed Lawler, a professor at the Center for Effective Organizations at the University of Southern California in Los Angeles, who says, "Line management should lead the effort, but HR has to be involved as a partner from the beginning."[30]

A spokesperson for Xerox, which won the Malcolm Baldrige National Quality Award in 1989, says that HR is an integral part of making quality a reality.[31] He states that HR professionals have two requirements to fulfill when their companies begin a quality program. They must ensure that:

1. All human resources subsystems — training, communication, and compensation — are aligned with the overall quality effort, and
2. The HR function is using quality principles.[32]

HR's Role in the Reengineering Process

Reengineering (or Business Process Redesign) is a hot topic in contemporary management in both the public and private sectors. As federal agencies confront management issues generated by downsizing, delayering, restructuring, etc., they have at their disposal a tool which is frequently referred to as business process reengineering (BPR). A recent NAPA study looking at government reengineering defines BPR as "a radical improvement approach that critically examines, rethinks, and redesigns mission product and service processes within a political environment. It achieves dramatic mission performance gains from multiple customer and stakeholder perspectives. It is a key part of a process management approach for optimal performance that continually evaluates, adjusts, or removes processes."[33] Achieving the optimum outcome from reengineering is heavily dependent on successful integration of human systems issues. This represents a significant new role for HR.

Because reengineering involves a myriad of HR challenges, Greengard believes it provides HR with a golden opportunity to put its stamp on an organization. Greengard quotes Janet Caldow, a senior consultant at the IBM Consulting Group: "It's up to HR to take the initiative and define its role. In most cases, things aren't clearly defined during a reengineering project. Those who step forward gain the opportunity to blaze the trail."[34]

The article discusses areas where HR can provide guidance and direction as a reengineering project unfolds. These include:
1. shaping the process,
2. creating job statements and role descriptions that reflect the new corporate order,
3. working out compensation issues,
4. training the new work force,
5. molding the new corporate culture, and
6. facilitating communication in the work force.[35]

Building HRM Capacity

HR must increase its capacity to perform in order to move from the current state to the desired state. The literature provides insights as to actions which can be taken to enhance HR's capacity. These include creating an appropriate HR organization design, matching staffing with performance requirements, developing HR staff skills, utilizing modern technology, and continually improving operations through benchmarking best practice organizations.

HR ORGANIZATION

Steers writes that organizational structure is driven by five building blocks.
- The first block contains individuals and groups and how they communicate, make decisions, show leadership, and handle power and organizational politics.
- Second are tasks and technology — what is the work to be done? Technology includes all tools used to get the job done such as guides, standards and knowledge, as well as automation.
- The third block includes organizational design — how the work is distributed and the relationships between various parts of the organization. Organizational design makes it possible for organizations to effectively coordinate and control work activities to achieve desired performance.
- Organizational processes are the fourth block. They determine how the work will actually be done.
- The final block is management. This is the glue which holds the other parts together. The success or failure of an organization, no matter how well designed, can hinge on the success of the management process.[36]

HR's Reporting Relationship

HR's reporting relationship to senior management is an important predictor of HR's potential to be involved in strategic planning and decision-making processes. Leibman and McManis note that having a seat at the management table is one crucial test of HR's perceived value in the organization.[37] A Towers Perrin/IBM survey of line managers, academicians, consultants, and HR executives found nearly universal agreement that

Literature Review Summary

HR heads should report to the CEO. The primary reason is to enable the HR head to link HR activities more closely to business strategies and goals.[38] Consistent with this view, King and Bishop note, "Being closer to the top signifies increased strategic importance and heightened expectations for HR to play a richer role in policy formulation as well as the more traditional clerical/audit and advisory roles HR plays."[39]

Filipowski and Halcrow found that in actual practice, the head of HR reporting to senior management is a fairly common practice in the top 100 U.S. corporations, with 58 percent of HR executives reporting to either the president or CEO.[40] The practice in the federal government is far less definitive. Some top HR positions are at the undersecretary level (e.g., DoD), assistant secretary (e.g., HHS), and deputy assistant secretary level (e.g., Navy, Army, and Interior). Many other top HR positions are several levels removed from the top executive. Those who do not report to the top officials tend to report to political executives in charge of management, administration or resource management.[41] The NPR did not address the issue of HR reporting channels.

To Centralize or Decentralize?

The merits of centralizing and decentralizing personnel operations have been debated for decades. The centralization advocates generally point to advantages of control and efficiency. The model for this approach is the General Motors organization under Alfred Sloan.[42] It is hard to argue with this model's success from the 1930s until 1980.

Historically, the federal government has opted to centralize staff functions in the name of efficiency and control.

Historically, the federal government has opted to centralize staff functions in the name of efficiency and control. For example, as a follow-on of the Grace Commission, case studies of shared administrative support were compiled for the President's Council on Management Improvement. Models held out for emulation included regional administrative support centers in the Departments of HHS, Labor and the Environmental Protection Agency.[43] Whether these approaches achieve efficiency without a loss of other potential benefits is not clear. In recent years, the move toward more decentralized models has gained momentum.

The literature indicates a trend toward a lessened role for central personnel organizations at the national government levels. The benefits of decentralizing work in organizations include: increased innovation and creativity; greater managerial efficiency and speed (decision making), more open communications and better feedback; job satisfaction; and employee retention.[44] The NPR supports this position and calls for delegating authority to the lowest practical level of line management.[45] But, the NPR is silent on how the HR support organization should structure to adjust, if at all, to support the needs of newly empowered line managers.

Some potential weaknesses to decentralization, include: more difficulty sharing the benefits of innovations across the organization; difficulties allocating pooled resources, such as computer support and purchasing; and the potential to suboptimize as each organization seeks to optimize its own goals at the expense of computer support and purchasing; and the potential to suboptimize as each organization seeks to optimize its own goals at the expense of broader goals. Decentralization can also impede the growth of competence and expertise due to inbreeding and isolation of skilled employees. Finally, decentralization, if not managed, can result in poor performance due to lack of high-level coordination and integration. Organizations which have reengineered their HRM processes have the ability to combine the advantages of centralization and decentralization in the same process. Information technology increasingly enables companies to operate as though their individual units were fully autonomous, while the organization still enjoys the economies of scale that centralization creates.[46]

The relationship of organizational structure to the cultural change envisioned by the NPR and required for TQM implementation is a key issue in organization design. Creech is one of the more passionate advocates of the need for a decentralized structure to enable successful implementation of TQM. He notes that, "it (TQM) must be based on a decentralized approach that provides empowerment at all levels, especially at the frontline, so that enthusiastic involvement and common purpose are realities, not slogans."[47] He also observes that centralized approaches deeply affect the psyche and spirit of employees to the detriment of organizational performance because centralism's excessive regulation depresses the human spirit.[48]

Generalists or Specialists?

The federal personnel system has been specialist-oriented for many years. This is driven, in part, by the structure and nature of the system. First, the Civil Service Commission (OPM) classification standards are organized around the personnel specialties — staffing, classification, employee relations, labor relations, training, and general personnel management.[49]

Second, the complex nature of the federal personnel management legal and regulatory structure requires personnel to know a significant body of information relating to each specified sub-function of the personnel system.[50] This forces people to specialize, out of necessity, to keep current with the rules governing any single area of HRM. Finally, OPM and most agency headquarters have organized their HR operations around personnel specialties, which then flow down to the operating level. Lower level HR organizations have modeled this structure which contributes to HR professionals communicating within the functional "stovepipe." Is this still the best way to organize the HR workforce in the year 2000 and beyond?

Hammer and Champy note that in the new world of work, units are changing from functional departments to process teams. "Companies are, in effect, putting back together again the work that Adam Smith and Henry Ford broke into tiny pieces."[51] Another dimension of Hammer's and Champy's analysis which has implications for the HR specialization issue is the trend toward jobs changing from simple tasks to multi-dimensional work. This trend affects the recruiting and skills development of HR practitioners. It also creates a need for more generalists working in "front room" operations with a limited number of specialists working in the "back room" who support the generalists when an especially complex issue is encountered.

Work is also changing to have a new focus on performance measures and compensation based on results rather than activities.[52] Specialists' work, by definition, is concerned with inputs and process because specialist work only involves a part of the whole. In many cases, specialists do not see the final output let alone the result. In the context of HR work, this suggests an exciting possibility with generalists helping managers

---

Literature Review Summary

The complex nature of the federal personnel management legal and regulatory structure requires personnel staff to know a significant body of information.

address issues or problems which cut across the HR functions, and seeing the final result in terms of organizational capacity improvement. It does not negate the need for a contingent of specialists who can assist with especially complex technical issues.

Improving Effectiveness and Efficiency

In the eyes of many managers and HR professionals, technology is the greatest hope for improved HR service and efficiency.[53] This perspective is becoming reality in DoD where HR is trying to maintain quality service while changing its traditional service delivery mechanisms to reduce the size of the HR staff.

In a presentation reported in the proceedings from an OPM conference held in June 1994, DoD representatives stated that DoD intends to "reduce its personnel staff from 15,000 to 10,000 and is aiming for a personnel servicing ratio of 1:100."[54] DoD plans to achieve this goal by consolidating HR services to all DoD components — Army, Navy, Air Force, and the Defense agencies — into a single organization. Furthermore, DoD is moving toward a regionalized configuration to deliver civilian personnel support. To accomplish these ambitious goals, DoD is relying heavily on state-of-the art automation systems.

The challenges facing federal HR offices are mirrored in the private sector. IBM's experiences in recent years are a case in point. To reduce costs while attempting to improve services, IBM created in 1991 a separate business within the corporate structure to handle HR services — Workforce Solutions (WFS). Its goals were to:

- continue to reduce the cost of personnel services;
- improve customer satisfaction and the quality of services;
- ensure flexibility to respond to the needs of business; and
- ensure state-of-the-art functional competence and innovation.[55]

WFS has reduced IBM's HR workforce from 1,700 to 950 (44 percent), while successfully executing its key role within the corporation.[56] WFS attributes its ability to reduce the size of the HR workforce while maintaining quality service to its ability to separate and implement both its strategic and tactical roles. That is a key difference between the private and public sectors. As discussed earlier, in the public sector the trend is more toward federal agencies accomplishing workforce reductions by targeting specific numbers rather than planning strategically.

WFS's HR staff reductions are not necessarily reflected in Bureau of National Affairs (BNA) figures on HR staff levels relative to the workforce within the private sector as a whole. BNA reports these figures to be virtually unchanged in recent years.[57] This apparent anomaly can be reconciled, at least in part, however, in light of the extensive overall workforce downsizing within the private sector over the past several years.

The median ratio of HR staff to total workforce is 1.0 staff members for every 100 employees in the workforce. This ratio varies with organizational size. As the workforce grows, the ratio declines from a median of 1.5 HR staff members per 100 workers in departments serving fewer than 250 workers, to just 0.5 per 100 among HR offices responsible for 2,500 or more employees.[58] These data reflect significant economies of scale for larger organizations. But, HR staffing must be considered in the context of functional scope, roles, performance and value added rather than simple ratios. The literature supports the notion of increased HR efficiency through reengineering, delegation of work, and automation. The danger is that preoccupation with simple measures and reduction targets will take precedence over capacity and performance of vital functions.

The executive round table offers another perspective on the issue of downsizing HR staffs. The executives agreed "that the HR profession's role and responsibilities are changing considerably as it moves from a corporate hiring and payroll function to a strategic business partner."[59] The executives predicted that HR departments will reduce in size as they increase their strategic influence. In addition, they see the current state of HR ceasing altogether as more traditional roles are "outsourced" to other departments or vendors. The article quoted a Rath & Strong vice president who said that "... The HR skill set is being spread out within organizations, with the trend toward smaller HR staff groups that are experts at managing change."[60]

Technology

The NPR clearly states that government needs to "expand the use of new technologies" in order to reengineer work.[61] Current government systems are inefficient and costly. In fact, "failure to adapt to the information age threatens many aspects of government."[62] Through investment in technology, the government can save time and reduce its staff. "Organizations don't need as many people collecting information because computers can do much of it automatically. They don't need as many people processing that information because clever software programs can give managers what they need at the press of a button."[63] In terms of HR, the government should follow the advice of the NPR by investing in new technologies that will achieve processing efficiencies and allow HR to become a strategic partner.

A human resources information system (HRIS) creates a bridge that connects HR professionals to strategic planning and enables HR to provide responsive services at reduced costs. The transformation is the result of a combination of powerful new computing technology with a reengineered organizational structure. Professionals in the field attest to this. According to William E. Berry, chairman of the West Palm Beach, Florida Consulting Team, Inc., "It [technology] is transforming human resources from a transaction-oriented entity into a department that can provide valuable insights into the workings and capabilities of the organization."[64]

An HRIS automates many functions that, in the past, bound HR to narrow process roles and creates innovative ways to gather, analyze, and disseminate information. "Imagine an HR information system with the following capabilities: It eliminates almost all paperwork; saves valuable staff time; allows employees to change benefits options, examines internal job postings and immediately bids for desired positions without assistance from HR personnel; and brings training, testing and management-by-objectives programs electronically to all company locations."[65] While not all organizations will create a system as powerful as Federal Express Corporation's described above, it is an example of the menu of options available today. These powerful systems are breaking down the walls between HR and the organization, which is paramount in developing a strategic planning partnership.

Literature Review Summary

Technology is transforming human resources from a transaction-oriented entity into a department that can provide valuable insights into the workings and capabilities of the organization.

Literature Review Summary

The HRIS manager is a vital link between an organization's personnel information and the way it is used in strategic planning. The HR role and the skills needed are changing due to new technology and new goals for reengineered HR organizations. "Now a new era is at hand, as the human resources function and its systems support have become strategic partners in managing change. With this evolutionary stage, as with the others, comes the need for HRIS management to learn new skills and competencies to remain assets to their organizations."[66] Timely and relevant workforce information is the ticket to the strategic planning party and a good HRIS system can provide the HR executive with the ticket.

An HRIS manager in an organization that is reorganizing, restructuring, and/or reengineering should realize that s/he is "a proactive participant in the management of business change and its HR implications . . . [and] should put additional competencies into their professional-development objectives in the 1990's."[67] An HRIS manager must:

- **Brainstorm innovative uses for new technology in his/her organization.**
  To do this, HRIS managers will need a broad, systems view of the organization and how their function can affect the entire organization.

- **Enhance communication skills.**
  HRIS managers must have better communication skills to remain abreast of changes within the organization and to suggest changes.

- **Have the ability to participate effectively in reengineering projects.**
  HRIS managers will provide the technical support for HR professionals in their role as change agents.

- **Understand the diverse HR needs.**
  HRIS must support a large variety of functions for a diverse staff.

- **Understand the core mission of the organization.**
  A broad perspective of the organization's mission will translate into an HRIS mission.

- **Ability to align HRIS with business goals and objectives.**
  To develop the technical support for on-going improvement efforts, HRIS managers must be aware of where the organization is going.[68]

An HRIS manager in a "reengineering organization" needs these characteristics and more; the individual must also have the proper outlook on technological innovation. Hammer and Champy believe HRIS managers must have a "reengineered mindset" towards technology. They contend that "throwing computers at an existing problem does not cause it to be reengineered."[69] First, one must learn how to think inductively. That is, an HRIS manager should, "first recognize a powerful solution and then seek the problems it might solve, problems the company probably doesn't even know it has."[70] In other words, one should not only consider implementing some new technology to improve procedures that already exist. They should consider the technology for something they are not doing.

Self-Service HR

An important feature of developing the HR department into a strategic partner is the ability to decentralize everyday functions. Through new self service systems, such as touch-tone phone systems and kiosks, workers can perform many standard personnel

An important feature of developing the HR department into a strategic partner is the ability to decentralize everyday functions.

functions. These systems can be used to update personal data (i.e., change of address, marital status), model benefits packages, post internal job openings and training opportunities, and publicize new policies. More sophisticated opportunities for manipulating information from self-service systems are increasingly accessible. Self-service accomplishes two major achievements: it further frees the HR specialists from routine tasks and manages/updates information so that they can perform analytical assignments needed by top management.

There are three categories of direct HR access: interactive voice response (IVR) systems, common access kiosks, and personal desktop computers.[71] Organizations' first self-service systems are usually IVR systems. Most often, IVRs are automatic phone answering/data collection systems similar to voice-mail or a recording at a credit card company. When an employee dials in, s/he follows instructions and uses the touch-tone keypad for data entry. In order to confirm the data, follow-up reports are sent via electronic mail, fax, or regular mail. Some distinct advantages to an IVR are that employees can update their records from anywhere, anytime; and a computer is not needed for input. Disadvantages include the lack of visible instructions and confusion with data entry when too many numbers must be entered. The advantages make the system attractive for simple changes or questions.

The cost savings of self service systems is a pivotal criterion for its use. Overburdened systems spend exorbitant amounts of money simply passing paper through the HR department. Self-service reduces costs because information does not change hands several times before being entered into the system, resulting in fewer mistakes. "... Self-service takes direct aim at the fattest target — HR administration — a function that soaks up 60 percent of HR costs, activities and headcount while adding only 10 percent in value."[72] According to Leckonby, "The beauty of HR companion applications is the ability to easily compare costs and benefits... they [HR professionals] need only to look at their operating budgets to find the raw data for analysis. The results of a study will quickly tell you which self-service applications give the highest rate of return."[73] Merck & Co. will save approximately $14.70 per data change through touch-tone phone services. They estimate 30,000 data changes this year, which will net the company $450,000 for their domestic workforce alone.[74] Although the cost savings are clear, it can be difficult for an organization to justify the initial investment.

BENCHMARKING AND HRM BEST PRACTICES

As federal agencies move toward implementing their HR reinvention objectives, they will have a number of tools available to choose from to help in this effort. Among these tools are TQM, process reengineering, and benchmarking. Benchmarking enables HR professionals to broaden their outlook concerning HR practices, incorporating the best practices of other organizations into their reinvention process.

The literature dealing with benchmarking in general, and benchmarking HR in particular, is primarily focused on the private sector. Benchmarking has increasingly gained popularity among private sector companies over the past 15 years as a method to examine best practices. Fitz-enz defines benchmarking as a management tool used by many organizations to investigate how others conduct certain processes.[75]

Literature Review Summary

Benchmarking enables HR professionals to broaden their outlook concerning HR practices, incorporating the best practices of other organizations into their reinvention process.

Literature Review Summary

Fitz-enz cautions that benchmarking can be misunderstood or misused. To clarify the meaning, he says the term can be used both as a noun and a verb. As a noun, a benchmark is a standard, a point of reference. It is not the same as a simple number, or what some call a metric. There is a difference between a comparative number, which may be the norm, and a benchmark, which is the best. As a verb, he describes benchmarking as a process. It is different from a group survey. Getting a group of people together to share data is not necessarily a benchmarking project. To qualify as a benchmarking project, one (or more) of the companies must be the benchmark — the standard to which others compare themselves. The benchmarks or references are two: the way the process is run and the results obtained from it.[76]

Federal agencies can find information about companies noted for HR best practices from publications publicized by firms specializing in benchmarking. Two such firms are Saratoga Institute's Human Resource Benchmark Network, which publishes an annual Human Resources Effectiveness Report, and HR Effectiveness Inc., which publishes the annual HR Best Practices Report.[77]

Measuring the Human Resources Management Function

Historically, organizations have done little to measure their HR functions.

Historically, organizations have done little to measure their HR functions. Considered a "soft" area, unlike production or sales, HR departments have been reluctant to be measured and organizations have been content to view HR as an expense center, overhead or just a necessary evil. However, organizations are looking more toward how HR provides value-added services. Managers want measures not only to know whether a function's productivity is improving, but also to be able to provide better information for decision making. Finally, managers want to be able to quantify information to justify additional resources and "increase the relevance of their operation to the organization."[78] Quality consultant James Harrington has stated: "The importance of measurement can't be overemphasized. If you can't measure it, you can't understand it. If you can't understand it, you can't control it. If you can't control it, you can't improve."[79]

There is no consensus on the key business ratios for a company's HR performance and potential. A 1990 survey of annual and 10K reports of some of the largest U.S. companies found mention of only a few HR indicators, and little standardization among those mentioned. More commonly cited were payroll and benefits per employee, number of employees, total assets per employee, and total sales per employee.[80] Another survey of the top HR professionals at Fortune 500 Industrial and Fortune 500 Service companies, conducted in 1992 by Hewitt Associates, found that, of the 151 companies responding: 93 percent measured benefits; 91 percent measured employee relations; 89 percent measured compensation; 79 percent measured employment/recruitment; 76 percent measured training; 68 percent measured strategic planning; and 43 percent measured work and family life.[81]

Carter has suggested how to measure both the functional areas of work completed in most HR departments and the overall effectiveness of the HR function.[82] The literature suggests that to develop those indicators, HR organizations should first determine what is important to the overall organization. According to Fitz-enz, the HR organization needs to know its internal customers' problems, goals, opportunities, pressures, and dreams in order to connect HR's services to its customer's needs.[83]

To hold its human resources development (HRD) departments accountable, GTE "puts its money where its training programs are." The department offers a money-back guarantee with every training program. The cost of training an employee comes out of the budget of the employee's department. The cost covers the delivery — materials, instructors, etc. If the employee is dissatisfied with the program, the HRD department will refund the money out of its own budget. To get the refund, the employee need only explain why s/he is unhappy.[84]

Fitz-enz states that the building blocks of measurement include processes, outputs, and impacts. HR processes can be measured along five indices of cost, time, quantity, quality, and human reaction (attitudes, morale, and/or customer satisfaction). Outputs can be measured in terms of how long did it take? How much did it cost? How much was done? What was the error rate? and how satisfied are the affected parties? Impact is measured in terms of the difference made by the output. For example, filling a position quickly might enable a manager to meet a deliverable deadline. Helping a manager deal with a problem employee might improve production and morale within the organization.[85]

CIVIL SERVICE REFORM

Government performance and accountability is an issue throughout the world. In its report, The World's Best Public Sector, the Finnish Ministry of Finance notes, "Several reforms of the public sector were made or attempted earlier, but the present wave of reform is thought of as particularly rigorous. In most Western countries, the present shake-up of the public sector is a profound, extensive and radical process."[86]

Ingraham and Romzek focus the drivers for reform by noting that the original design of the public service was intended to solve problems with employees who lacked skills and acquired their jobs through patronage. Today, the problems are different, and are characterized by inflexibility, eroding capacity and legitimacy, and overemphasis on process rather than outcomes.[87] Reforms in western market economies are being propelled by a general prejudice against the concept of state, a response to the crisis of the welfare state, budget deficits, and a public cry to reduce the role of government and find delivery sources which are more responsive.[88]

The substance of the reforms has been directed toward cost reduction and increased productivity, shifting emphasis from inputs and process to results and personal accountability, a reassessment of the public sector's role and function, and selective use of market mechanisms and increased incentives.[89] The reforms demand a change in public organizations' culture, stressing a customer orientation, results orientation, measurement, decentralization of authority, and the empowerment of managers and line employees.[90]

The civil service's importance to the success of overall government reform efforts is generally acknowledged. The Organisation for Economic Co-operation and Development (OECD) notes, "even the most obvious proposals for change are meaningless if people cannot be made to implement them."[91] OECD also states that many countries consider developing personnel management the main challenge to changing over to a new style

Several reforms of the public sector were made or attempted earlier, but the present wave of reform is thought of as particularly rigorous.

Literature Review Summary

of government.[92] The civil service personnel system must lead to a workforce which is skilled/competent, service minded, and well trained (maintaining skills throughout their careers).[93]

The roles of central management agencies are undergoing a major change: from directing and issuing instructions to managing by agreement, with greater departmental discretion to make substantive decisions. Binding regulations are giving way to more consultative approaches.[94] Mascarenhas reports that reforms in Australia, Britain and New Zealand have been based on public choice regarding public services. The reforms' main objectives were to bring about efficiency in the public sector by giving departmental heads total autonomy and responsibility for managing departments and then holding them accountable for performance.[95]

British reforms have reasserted the minister's role for policy making and given department heads responsibility for managing their departments. Department heads' management authority resides within the defining standards and principles of the civil service, which continues to be centrally prescribed and mandatory. Some delegation of pay and grading authority below the senior level has been made and more delegation in this area has been proposed. To achieve further improvement in civil service performance, a proposal has been made to increase the focus on performance management and employee training. Also under consideration are changes to the senior civil service including new pay systems, succession planning and written employment contracts, which might include fixed term and rolling contracts.[96]

The New Zealand government adopted a system of contractual appointments and performance agreements along the lines of the private sector for its departmental chief executives. Of particular interest to the current U.S. civil service reform is New Zealand's decision to essentially abolish the central personnel agency as it existed, and allow public managers to adopt personnel systems which fit their needs. In doing so, public managers follow the same rules as private sector employers. These reforms have generated some lessons learned, including that management autonomy works better at the operational level than at the policy level, where politics is one of the principal, if not primary, considerations. Another lesson is that without some central integration suboptimization can occur as each department strives to optimize its particular set of efficiency and service measures without considering the impacts on other jurisdictions.[97]

The National Commission on the State and Local Public Service published a report in 1993 which defines the state of the public service at levels below the national government. The report Hard Truths/Tough Choices (also known as the Winter Report), noted a growing consensus that state and local governments need to drastically improve their capacity and performance. Governments hamstring their chief executives by diffusing their power, and asking them to operate with antiquated and obsolete procurement, budget, and personnel systems. In addition, they fail to invest in the most critical resource they have: the rank and file personnel.[98] The report calls for a wide range of actions to improve the performance of state and local jurisdictions including:

- strengthening executive authority in a number of areas,
- flattening the bureaucracy,

- deregulating government by reforming the civil service, including eliminating veterans preference and seniority,
- creating a learning government by restoring employee training and education budgets,
- basing pay increases on skills, not seniority,
- changing the role of managers to problem solvers instead of paper passers, and
- encouraging a new style of labor-management communication.[99]

The NPR is quite similar to other public reform efforts around the world. The overall theme is "a government which works better and costs less." The strategy is to:
- Put the customer first by establishing customer service standards, and using modern technology to enhance service delivery.
- Empower employees to get results. This is to be accomplished through partnerships with employee unions and reducing supervisory, managerial, and support staffs who are perceived as interfering with line employee effectiveness.
- Cut red tape by eliminating excessive rules and reforming management systems for procurement, financial management and personnel.
- Get back to basics by reducing the federal deficit and spending available funds more effectively (eliminate marginal or obsolete programs).[100]

Much has been done over the years to reform the civil service throughout the world. The pace and extent of change currently underway is perhaps unprecedented. There is much to be learned by the experience of others in this area, but the pressure for quick change and results is apparent. In the context of history, it would seem that the current efforts are but a step along the path to a better public service. It is unlikely that the NPR is the "end all and be all," and implementation of the evolutionary changes outlined in the NPR should look to the future when more dramatic changes may be necessary and politically possible.

ENDNOTES

1. Fitz-enz, Jac, *Human Value Management*, Jossey-Bass: San Francisco, 1990, 7.
2. Ibid., 9.
3. U.S. Department of Labor, "High Performance Work Practices and Firm Performance," 1993, 10-11.
4. Kravetz, Dennis, *The Human Resources Revolution*, Jossey-Bass: San Francisco, 1988, 11, in U.S. Department of Labor, High Performance Work Practices and Firm Performance, Government Printing Office: Washington, D.C. August 1993.
5. Ulrich, Dave and Arthur Yeung, "A Shared Mindset," *Personnel Administrator*, March 1989, 38.
6. National Performance Review, *Creating a Government that Works Better and Costs Less, Reinventing Human Resources Management, Accompanying Report to the National Performance Review*, September 1993, 4.
7. Schay, Brigitte, "Criteria for Effective HRM Programs," Briefing to Institute for International Research, September 24, 1994.
8. Carter, Carla C., "Measuring and Improving the Human Resources Function," *Employment Relations Today*, v21n1, Spring 1994, 73-74.

Literature Review Summary

9. Merit Systems Protection Board (MSPB), Federal Personnel Offices: Time For Change? Merit Systems Protection Board: Washington, D.C., August 30, 1992, 9.
10. National Academy of Public Administration, *Revitalizing Federal Management: Managers and Their Overburdened Systems,* 1983, 38.
11. Op. Cit., Fitz-enz, *Human Value Management,* 119-123.
12. HR Effectiveness Inc., *Borrowing from the Best: HR Best Practices 1993 Annual Report,* Beaverton, Oregon, 10-11, 13.
13. D. McGregor, "The Staff Function in Human Relations," *Journal of Social Issues,* Summer 1948, 8.
14. Ibid., 277-282.
15. President's Council on Management Improvement, *Improving the Management of Human Resources in the Federal Government Through a Private-Public Partnership,* vI, PCMI: Washington, D.C., 1987.
16. National Academy of Public Administration (NAPA), *Revitalizing Federal Management: Managers and their Overburdened Systems,* 1983, 38.
17. Op. Cit., NPR, OPM Accompanying Report, 1.
18. Office of Personnel Management, *Personnel and Oversight Group Survey of Federal Employees,* Office of Personnel Management: Washington, D.C., May 1992, 1, 10.
19. Merit Systems Protection Board (MSPB), *Federal Personnel Offices: Time For Change?* Merit Systems Protection Board: Washington, D.C., August 30, 1992, ix, 38.
20. Ibid., 33.
21. Steers, Richard M., *Introduction to Organizational Behavior,* Harper Collins: New York, 1991, 486-487.
22. Bureau of National Affairs, Human *Resources Activities, Budgets, and Staffs: 1993-94, SHRM-BNA Survey No. 59,* June 30, 1994, 1-16.
23. Ibid., p. 1. This figure demonstrates that HR responsibilities are seldom static. This is the third year in a row that about one-third of the organizations surveyed by SHRM-BNA reported changes in HR responsibilities. See Bureau of National Affairs, Inc., Human Resources Activities, Budgets, and Staffs: 1992-93, SHRM-BNA Survey No. 58, May 27, 1993, 1, and Bureau of National Affairs, Inc., Human Resources Activities, Budgets, and Staffs: 1991-92, SHRM-BNA Survey No. 57, June 25, 1992, 1.
24. Ibid., 3-6.
25. Ibid., 5.
26. Ibid., 6.
27. Ulrich, Dave, "A New HR Mission: Guiding the Quality Mindset," *HR Magazine,* December 1993, 51.
28. Roth, William F., "Quality, an Opportunity for Human Resources," *The Total Quality Review,* May/June 1994, 9.
29. Caudron, Shari, "How HR Drives TQM," *Personnel Journal,* August 1993, 48B.
30. Ibid., 48B.
31. Ibid., 48D.
32. Ibid., 48F.
33. National Academy of Public Administration, Center for Information Management, *Reengineering for Results: Keys to Success from Government Experience,* August 1994, xi.
34. Ibid., xi.
35. Ibid., xi.
36. Op. Cit., Steers, 20-22.
37. Op. Cit., Leibman and McManis, 30.
38. Op. Cit., Towers Perrin, 44.
39. King, Albert S. and Terrence Bishop, "Human Resources Experience: Survey and Analysis," *Public Personnel Management,* Spring 1994, 168.
40. Filipowski, Diane and Allan Halcrow, "HR Leaders Are Powerful," *Personnel Journal,* December 1992, 48.
41. Information based on a review of the organization structure listed in federal phone directory.
42. Op. Cit., Steers, 311.
43. President's Council on Management Improvement, "New Perspectives on Federal Management-Case Studies of Shared Administrative Support," Washington D.C., 1985.
44. Ibid., 311.

45. Op. Cit., NPR *HRM Accompanying Report*, 25.
46. Hammer, Michael and James Champy, *Reengineering the Corporation,* Harper Collins: New York, 1993, 63.
47. Creech, Bill, "The Five Pillars of TQM," Truman/Talley: New York, 1994, 5.
48. Ibid., 11.
49. U.S. Civil Service Commission, see various classification standards for GS-200 series positions.
50. Ibid., NPR *HRM Accompanying Report,* see various sections related to overregulation in federal HRM.
51. Op. Cit., Hammer and Champy, 65.
52. Ibid., 72.
53. Ibid., 25.
54. Office of Personnel Management, "Partners for Change: June 1-2 Conference Proceedings," September 1994, 27.
55. Ibid., 19.
56. Ibid., 20.
57. Op. Cit., Bureau of National Affairs, 8-9.
58. Ibid., 1.
59. "The Future of HR: Smaller Staffs and Greater Influence," *HR Focus,* June 1993, 5.
60. Ibid., 5.
61. Op. Cit., NPR, 112.
62. Ibid., 113.
63. Ibid., 112.
64. Greengard, Samuel, "The Next Generation," *Personnel Journal,* 41.
65. Palvia, Prashant, Sherry Sullivan and Steven Zeltman, "Prism Profile: An Employee-Oriented System," *HR Focus,* June 1993, 19.
66. Pasqualetto, Joe, "HRIS Has Evolved from Capturing Information to Managing Change," *Personnel Journal,* January 1993, 92.
67. Joe Pasqualetto, "New Competencies Define the HRIS Manager's Future Role," *Personnel Journal,* 99.
68. Ibid., 99.
69. Op. Cit., Hammer and Champy, 83.
70. Ibid., 84-85.
71. Hare, Jonathan, "Do it yourself HR," *Benefits and Compensation Solutions,* 35.
72. Ibid., 34.
73. Leckonby, William R., "Streamline Your HR Services with Kiosks," *HR Focus,* May 1993, 18.
74. Op. Cit., Hare, 34.
75. Fitz-enz, Jac, "How to Make Benchmarking Work for You," *HR Magazine,* December 1993, 40.
76. Ibid., 41.
77. Ibid., Fitz-enz, 47.
78. Op. Cit., Carter, 63.
79. Fitz-enz, Jac, "HR's New Score Card," *Personnel Journal,* February 1994, 86.
80. Hansson, Robert O., Nancy D. Smith and Pamela S. Mancinelli, "Monitoring the HR Job Function," *HR Magazine,* February 1990, 76.
81. Hewitt Associates, *HR's Strategic Role in Building Competitiveness,* 1992, 2.
82. Op. Cit., Carter, 63-75.
83. Op. Cit., Fitz-enz, "HR's New Score Card," 89.
84. Op. Cit., Steinburg, 34.
85. Op. Cit., Fitz-enz, *Human Value Management,* 286-290.
86. Ministry of Finance, "The World's Best Public Sector?" Finland, 45.
87. Ingraham, Patricia and Barbara S. Romzek & Associates, *New Paradigms for Government,* Jossey-Bass: San Francisco, 1994, 332.
88. Op. Cit., Ministry of Finance, 46-50.
89. Ibid., 54.

90. Ibid., 56.
91. Ibid., 70.
92. Ibid., 76
93. Ibid., 58.
94. Ibid., 63.
95. Mascarenhas, R.C., "Building an Enterprise Culture in the Public Sector in Australia, Britain and New Zealand," *Public Administration Review,* July/August 1993, 326-327.
96. The Prime Minister, The Chancellor of the Exchequer and the Chancellor of the Duchy of Lancaster, "The Civil Service-Continuity and Change," A White Paper presented to theParliament, July 1994, 1-4.
97. Sherwood, Frank P., "Comprehensive Government Reform in New Zealand," *The Public Manager,* Spring 1992, 23.
98. National Commission on the State and Local Public Service, *Hard Truths/Tough Choices,* The Nelson Rockefeller Institute of Government: Albany, New York, 1993, 1.
99. Ibid., 4.
100. Ibid., 4.

BIBLIOGRAPHY

Albrecht, Karl, "At America's Service," Warner Books: New York, 1988.

Anthony, Peg, "Link HR to Corporate Strategy," *Personnel Journal,* April 1991, 75-86.

Auditor General of Canada Chapter Six, *Report of the Auditor General of Canada to the House of Commons,* Ottawa, Canada, 1993.

Australian Public Service Commission PSC Annual Report 1992-1993, Australian Government Publishing Service, Canberra, 1993.

Bailey, Betty, "Ask What HR Can Do for Itself," *Personnel Journal,* v70n7, July 1991, 35-39.

Ball, Gordon, "The Spartan Profession," *Personnel Management,* v24n9, September 1992.

Bamberger, Peter and Bruce Phillips, "Organization Environment and Business Strategy: Parallel vs Conflicting Influences on HR Strategy in the Pharmaceutical Industry," *Human Resource Management,* v30n2, Summer 1991.

Barr, Stephen, "Midterm Exam for 'Reinventing'," *The Washington Post,* August 18, 1994.

Belasco, James, "Building a Customer-Focused, Quality-Based Organization," U.S. Chamber of Commerce, San Diego, California, May 17, 1994.

Bellman, Geoff, "20 Thoughts on Dealing with Management," *Training and Development Journal,* April 1979.

Benefits & Compensation International, "16th IIHR Conference: New Orleans," v22n10, June 1983.

Benowitz, Stephen C. and Susan N. Hill, "A Model for HRM at the National Institutes of Health — Draft," Bethesda, Maryland, January 16, 1994.

Benowitz, Stephen C., "New Age Personnel-Quality Service Delivery in Changing Times," *Public Personnel Management,* v23n2, Summer 1994, 181185.

Berridge, John, "Human Resource Management in Britain," *Employee Relations,* v14n5, 1992.

Blackburn, Richard and Benson Rosen, "Total Quality and Human Resources Management: Lessons Learned from Baldrige AwardWinning Companies," *Executive,* v7n3, August 1993.

Boroski, John W., "Putting It Together: HR Planning in "3D" at Eastman Kodak," *Human Resource Planning,* v13n1, 1990.

Bournois, Frank and Veronique Torchy, "HRM in Financial Services Organizations: France and Britain Compared," *European Management Journal,* v10n3, September 1992.

Brookes, Donald, "Merit Pay: Does it Help or Hinder Productivity?," *HR Focus,* v70n1, January 1993, 13.

Brookler, Rob, "What Hardware Means to the HRIS," *Personnel Journal,* v71n5, May 1992, 122-138.

Brown, Donna, "HR: Survival Tool for the 1990s," Management Review, March 1991.

Bureau of Business Practices, Excellence Achieved in Human Resources Management: Blueprints for Action From 61 Leading Companies, Bureau of Business Practice, 1991.

Burke, W. Warner and Allan H. Church, "Managing Change, Leadership Style, and Intolerance to Ambiguity: A Survey of Organization Development Practitioners," *Human Resource Management*, v31n4, Winter 1992, 301-317.

Business Europe, "Why France's LVMH Sets Common HR Rules," *Business Europe*, v33n43, November 8, 1993.

Business Horizons, "The Light at the End of the HRM Tunnel: Window of Opportunity or An Oncoming Train," *Business-Horizons*, January 1993.

Butteris, Margaret and Bob Osborne, "HR Program at Ontario Hydro," *Employee Relations*, v13n6.

Cameron, Kim S., "Strategies for Successful Organizational Downsizing," *Human Resource Management*, v33n2, Summer 1994.

Cardillo, Robin C., "Riding the Compensation Bandwagon," *Financial Executive*, MarchApril 1994, 78.

Carruthers, Gary, Motivating the Bureaucracy Draft.

Carter, Carla C., "Measuring and Improving the Human Resources Function," *Employment Relations Today*, v21n1, Spring 1994, 63-75.

Caudle, Sharon L., "Managing Information Technology for Results," *The Public Manager*, The Bureaucrat, Inc.: Arlington, VA, Spring 1994.

Caudron, Shari, "Change Keeps TQM Programs Thriving," *Personnel Journal*, October 1993, 104-109.

———, "Contingent Work Force Spurs HR Planning," *Personnel Journal*, July 1994, 52-60.

———, "How Celestial Seasoning is Preparing for Growth," *Personnel Journal*, v7n11, November 1993.

———, "How HR Drives TQM," *Personnel Journal*, August 1993.

Champy, James, "Reengineering," Across the Board, June 1993, 27-33.

Cipolla, Frank P., *Future of the Civil Service*, Kansas City, June 3, 1994.

———, "Forum – Issues for the 90's," *The Bureaucrat*, Summer 1991.

———, "Federal Executive Turnover: Crisis or Opportunity?," *The Public Manager*, Spring 1993, 25-27.

Coleman, Wayne A., *Compensation Trends, Classification and Compensation*, Washington, D.C., July/August 1994.

Collins, Brett and Adrian Payne, "Internal Marketing: A New Perspective for HRM," *European Management Journal*, v9n3, September 1991.

Consortium For Culture Change Handout, Change Inaugural Conference, Marvin Center, George Washington University, September 20, 1994.

Conference Board Human Resources Management Material, Conference Board, January 25, 1994.

Conner, Daryl R., *Positioning Human Resources as a Strategic Resource*, 1990.

Connock, Stephen, "The Importance of "Big Ideas" to HR Managers," *Personnel Management*, v24n6, June 1992.

Cooke, Roger and Michael Armstrong, "The Search for Strategic HRM," *Personnel Management*, v22n12, December 1990, 30-33.

Correia, Kathleen, "Get into the Outsourcing Loop," *HR Focus*, v71n4, April 1994, 15.

Council of Competitiveness, *Elevating the Skills of the American Workforce*, Council of Competitiveness, 1993.

Creech, Bill, "The Five Pillars of TQM," Truman/Talley: New York, 1994, 5.

Crupi, Dr. James A., Human Resources Slides, Strategic Leadership Solutions.

Csoka, Louis S., *Everything You Ever Wanted to Know About HRM But Were Afraid to Ask*, The Conference Board Presentation, January 11, 1994.

Davis, Vicki S., "Self-audits: First Step in TQM," *HR Magazine*, September 1992, 39-41.

Devanna, Mary Anne and Noel Tichy, "Creating the Competitive Organization of the 21st Century: The Boundaryless Corporation," *Human Resource Management*, v29n4, Winter 1990.

Development Dimensions International Making Reengineering Work: Integrating the Human Side of Reengineering, Sixth International PEPI Conference Reengineering Forum.

DiIulio, John J. and Gerald Garvey, *Improving Government Performance: An Owner's Manual*, Brookings Institution, Washington, D.C.

Dodson, Robert L., "Quality Means Customer Accountability," *HR Magazine*, v36n5, May 1991, 135-136.

Donnelly, Kate and Peter V. LeBlanc, "Career Banding," *Human Resource Management*, v31n1, Spring/Summer 1992.

Literature Review Summary

Douglas, James E., "The Executive Information System: A Power Drill for HR Data," *Human Resources Professional*, v4n4, Summer 1992.

Drucker, Peter F., "The Age of Social Transformation," *The Atlantic Monthly*, November 1994, 62-72.

Dubnick, Melvin J. and Barbara S. Romzek, "Issues of Accountability in Flexible Personnel Systems," in Patricia W Ingraham and Barbara S. Romzek, eds, *New Paradigms for Government*, Jossey-Bass: San Francisco, 1994.

Dyer, Lee and Gerald W. Holder, *A Strategic Perspective of Human Resources Management*, Bureau of National Affairs: Washington, D.C., 1988, 33-34.

Elliott, Vicki and Anna Orgera, "Competing for and With Workforce 2000," *HR Focus*, v70n6, June 1993.

Ettorre, Barbara and Catherine Romano, "AMA's HR Conference Report — Reengineering: The HR Perspective," *HR Focus*, v71n6, June 1994, 3-6.

Fabi, Bruno and Normand Pettersen, "Human Resource Management Practices in Project Management," *International Journal of Project Management*, v10n2, May 1992.

Fay, Carol and et. al., "When Success in a Habit," The *Public Manager*, The Bureaucrat, Inc.: Arlington, VA, Spring 1994.

Federal Aviation Administration, FAA *HRM Business Plan Briefing*, October 26, 1994, 23.

———, *Reinventing Human Resource Management in FAA*, Federal Aviation Administration Business Plan,, Washington, D.C., October 29, 1993.

Federal Quality Institute, *Criteria for the Presidential Award for Quality*, Office of Personnel Management, Washington, D.C., June 1993.

Filipowski, Diane, "Alergan's Structuring for Success," *Personnel Journal*, v70n3, March 1991.

Filipowski, Diane and Allan Halcrow, "HR Leaders Are Powerful," *Personnel Journal*, December 1992, 48.

———, "Who are the Leaders in HR at the Nation's Largest Publicly and Privately Held Companies?," *Personnel Journal*, December 1992.

Fitch, Vernon and et. al., "1994 Society for Human Resources Management and CCH Survey," *CCH Human Resources Management*, CCH, Inc.: Chicago, IL, June 22, 1994.

Fitzenz, Jac, *Human Value Management*, JosseyBass, Inc.: Washington, D.C., 1990.

———, *Benchmarking Staff Performance*, JosseyBass, Inc.: Washington, D.C., 1993.

———, "How to Make Benchmarking Work For You," *HR Magazine*, December 1993, 40-47.

———, "HR's New Score Card," *Personnel Journal*, v73n2, February 1994, 84-91.

Flander, Gail, "Out of Chaos, Opportunity," *Personnel Journal*, v73n3, March 1994, 83-88.

Flynn, Gillian, "A New HRIS in Sake County Streamlines HR," *Personnel Journal*, v73n5, May 1994, 137-142.

———, "DOL Requests Funding for Reinvention," *Personnel Journal*, June 1994, 125.

Foster, Lawrence W., *Advances in Applied Business Strategy, 1991: A Research Annual*, 1991.

Fox, Mary Jayne, *Furniture Dealer Links Payroll with Human Resources*, Office of Technology Management, v26n7, January 1992.

Franklin, Daniel, "Downsizing: Is it Aimed at the Right Targets?," *The Washington Monthly*, November 1994, 22-27.

Frohman, Mark and Alan L. Frohman, "Organization Adaptation: A Personnel Responsibility," *Personnel Administrator*, January 1994, 45-47, 88, 90.

Frick, Ken, "Natural Resources," *Bank Systems and Technology*, September 1993.

Frye, Colleen, "HR Looks Toward Future," *Software Magazine*, v12n16, November 1992.

Galbraith, Jay, "Positioning HR as a Value-adding Function: The Case of Rockwell International," *Human Resource Management*, v31n4, Winter 1992, 287-300.

Galves, Al, "Seeing Problems Eye to Eye," *Human Resources Professional*, v7n2, March/April 1994.

Garavan, Thomas N., "Strategic Human Resource Development," *International Journal of Manpower*, v12n6, 1991.

———, "Strategic Human Resource Development," *Journal of European Industrial Training*, v15, 1991.

Gibson, Virginia M., "Outsourcing Can Save Money and Increase Efficiency," *HR Focus*, v70n3, March 1993.

Gilbert, Ronald G., "Human Resource Management Practices to Improve Quality: A Case Example of Human Resource Management Intervention in Government," *Human Resource Management*, Summer 1991, v302n2, 183-198.

Glanz, Ellen F. and Lee K. Dailey, "Benchmarking," *Human Resource Management,* 9-20.

Godard, John, "The Progressive HRM Paradigm: A Theoretical and Empirical Re-examination," *Industrial Relations,* Quebec, Spring.

Goodsir, Jane, "A New Beat for HR in the Police," *Personnel Management,* v25n12, December 1993.

Gonzalez-Angueson, Luis, "World-Class Management," *HR Magazine,* v37n5, May 1992, 128, 126.

Griffiths, Ward, "A Leaner, Fitter Future for HR?," *Personnel Management,* v25n10, October 1993.

Greengard, Sammuel, "The Next Generation," *Personnel Journal,* March 1994, 40-46.

———, "Reengineering: Out of the Rubble," *Personnel Journal,* December 1993, 48B-48O.

Gunnigle, Patrick, "Personnel Policy Choice: The Context for Human Resource Development," *Journal of European Industrial Training,* v15, 1991.

Gupta, Ashok K. and Arvind Singhal, "Managing Human Resources for Innovation and Creativity," *Research and Technology Management,* May-June 1993, 41-48.

HR Effectiveness, Inc., *HR Best Practices: 1993 Annual Report,* HR Effectiveness, Inc., Beaverton, Oregon, 1993.

HR Focus, "More Companies Would Rather Outtask than Outsource," *HR Focus,* v71n4, April 1994.

———, "The Future of HR: Smaller Staffs and Greater Influence," *HR Focus,* v70n6, June 1993, 5.

HR News, "Job Evaluations Recommended for CEOs, Boards," *HR News,* August 1994.

HRM Strategies, Inc., *The HR Strategies 1991 Survey of Human Resources Trends,* October 1991.

HR Magazine, "Managing in the Leaner Organization," *HR Magazine,* November 1992, 3943.

Halcrow, Allan, "Optimas Reflects Changes in HR," *Personnel Journal,* January 1994, 50-64.

Hall, James L., *Federal Personnelist Employment Trends 1969-1991,* U.S. Office of Personnel Management Office of Workforce Information.

Hamel, Gary and C.K. Prahalad, "Strategic Intent, Gaining Strategic Advantage," *Harvard Business Review,* May/June 1988.

Hammer, Michael and James Champy, *Reengineering the Corporation,* Harper Collins: New York, 1993, 63.

Hammer, Michael, "The Age of Reengineering," *Across the Board,* June 1993.

———, "Reengineering Work: Don't Automate, Obliterate," *Harvard Business Review,* July/August 1990, 104-112.

Hansson, Robert O., Nancy D. Smith and Pamela S. Mancinelli, "Monitoring the HR Job Function," *HR Magazine,* v35n2, February 1990, 76-78.

Hare, Jonathan, "Do it Yourself HR," *Benefits and Compensation Solutions,* 34-37.

Hart, Christopher, "Total Quality Management and the Human Resource Professional: Applying the Baldrige Framework to Human Resources," *Human Resource Management,* 433-454.

Harper, Kirke, "Trends in Management Education," *The Public Manager,* The Bureaucrat, Inc.: Arlington, VA, Spring 1994.

Hart, Christopher and Leonard Schlesinger, "Total Quality Management and the Human Resource Professional: Applying the Baldrige Framework to Human Resources," *Human Resource Management,* Winter 1991, 433-454.

Hazucha, Joy Fisher and Sarah A. Hezlett, "The Impact of 360-degree Feedback on Management Skills Development," *Human Resource Management,* Summer/Fall 1993.

Heilemann, John, "Uncivil Service," *Best of Business Quarterly,* Summer 1991, 68-74.

Hendry, Chris and Andrew Pettigrew, "Patterns of Strategic Change in the Development of HRM," *British Journal of Management,* v3n3, September 1992.

Herbig, Paul and Fred Palumbo, "Total Quality and the Human Resource Professional," *TQM Magazine,* v6n2, 1994.

Hewitt Associates, *HR's Strategic Role in Building Competitiveness,* Hewitt Associates, 1992.

Hix, William M. and Ronald E. Sorter, *Strategic Planning for the United States Army Personnel Function,* Rand Corporation, Santa Monica, CA, 1991.

Hoogendoorn, Jacob, "New Priorities for Dutch HRM," *Personnel Management,* v24n12, December 1992.

Horner, Constance, "Deregulating the Federal Service: Is the Time Finally Right?," *Brookings Review,* Fall 1993, 24-27.

Human Resources *Development Division Consulting Guide for the Human Resources Professional,* Department of Transportation, Washington, D.C.

Literature Review Summary

Hunt, Michele, "The Quality Hunt," *Government Executive,* April 1994.

Huselid, Mark, "The Impact of Human Resource Management Practices on Turnover, Productivity, and Corporate Financial Performance," *Academy of Management Journal,* May 1, 1994.

IBM Workforce Solutions: Human Resources Materials, IBM.

Industrial Relations Review, "Institute of Manpower Studies Devolving Personnel Duties to Line Managers," *Industrial Relations Review & Report,* n560, May 1994.

———, "Union Responses to New Management Practices Surveyed," *Industrial Relations Review & Report,* n523, November 1992.

Ingraham, Patricia W. and Barbara S. Romzek & Associates, *New Paradigms for Government,* Jossey-Bass: San Francisco, 1994.

Ingraham, Patricia W. and Donald F. Kettl, *An Agenda for Excellence in America,* Chatham House Publishers: Chatham, N.J., 1992.

Ingraham, Patricia W. and David H. Rosenbloom, "The State of Merit in the Federal Government," *National Committee on the Public Service,* June 1990.

Jasper, Herbert N., Alpern, Anita F., "National Performance Review: The Good, the Bad, the Indifferent," *The Public Manager,* Spring 1994, 27-34.

Jenkins, Kate and Karen Caines, *Improving Management in Government: The Next Steps,* London, U.K., 1991.

Johns Hopkins University, *Hopkins Fellows in Change Management: An Intensive Program in Change Management for Organizational Leaders,* Johns Hopkins University: Baltimore, Maryland.

Johnston, William B. and et. al., Prepared for Office of *Personnel Management, Civil Service 2000,* Government Printing Office: Washington, D.C., June 1988.

Kanin-Lovers, Jill and David Miller, "Adopting a Simple Framework," *Journal of Compensation & Benefits,* v9n4, January/February 1993.

Kass, Rochelle, "Natural Resources," *Bank Systems & Technology,* v30n9, September 1993.

Kaufman, Bruce E., "What Companies Want from HR Graduates," *HR Magazine,* September 1994.

Keller, Deborah A. and John Campbell, "Building Human Resource Capability," *Human Resource Management,* v31n1, Spring/Summer 1992, 109-126.

Kemper, Gary W., "Managing Corporate Communication in Turbulent Times: Partnering with HR," *Communication World,* v9n5, May/June 1992.

Kettl, Donald F., *Reinventing Government? Appraising the National Performance Review,* Brookings Institution, Washington, D.C., 1994.

King, Albert S. and Terrence R. Bishop, "Human Resource Experience: Survey and Analysis," *Public Personnel Management,* v23n1, Spring 1994.

Kinnie, N.J. and R.V.W Staughton, "Implementing Manufacturing Strategy: The Human Resource Management Contribution," *Logistics Information Management,* v6n2, 1993.

Koch, Kathleen Day and Paul Ellis, "Protesting Whistleblowers," *The Public Manager,* The Bureaucrat, Inc.: Arlington, VA, Spring 1994.

Kochanski, James and Phillip M. Randall, "Rearchitecting the HR function at Northern Telecom," *Human Resources Management,* v33n2, Summer 1994.

Koons, Paul F., "Getting Comfortable with TQM," *The Bureaucrat,* Summer 1991, 35-38.

Kravetz, Dennis, *The Human Resources Revolution,* Jossey-Bass: San Francisco, 1988.

Kromling, Larry K., "CalComp Considers HR a Business Unit," *Personnel Journal,* v72n2, February 1993.

Kydd, Christine T. and Lynn Oppenheim, "Using Human Resource Management to Enhance Competitiveness: Lessons from Four Excellent Companies," *Human Resource Management,* Summer 1990.

———, "Using HRM to Enhance Competitiveness: Lessons from Four Excellent Companies," *Human Resource Management,* v29n2, Summer 1990.

Laabs, Jennifer J., "Successful Outsourcing Depends on Critical Factors," *Personnel Journal,* v72n10, October 1993.

———, "Why HR is Turning to Outsourcing," *Personnel Journal,* v72n9, September 1993.

Laurie, John, "The ABCs of Change Management," *Training and Development Journal,* March 1990, 87-89.

Leckonby, William, "Streamline Your HR Services," *HR Focus,* May 1993, 18.

Lee, Quarterman, "Quality in the Balance," *The Quality Observer,* April 1994, 3, 4 & 19.

Leonard, Bill, "Outsourcing Relocation Services — Are HR Managers Cutting Their Own Throats?," *HR Magazine,* v38n12, December 1993.

Leibman, Michael S., "Getting Results from TQM," *HR Magazine,* September 1992, 34-38.

Leibman, Michael S. and Gerald McManis, "HR's Value to the Business," *Personnel Administrator,* March 1989, 30-32.

Levine, Charles and Rosslyn Kleeman, *The Quiet Crisis of the Civil Service: The Federal Personnel System at the Crossroads,* National Academy of Public Administration, December 1986.

Light, Paul, "Do We Still Need an OPM?," *HR Magazine,* February 1994, 51-53.

Li-Ping Tang, Thomas, Peggy Smith Tollison and Harold D. Whiteside, "Differences Between Active and Inactive Quality Circles in Attendance and Performance," *Public Personnel Management,* Winter 1993, 579-590.

Losey, Michael, R., "Committing to Lifelong Excellence," *HR Magazine,* v38n8, August 1993, 108-110.

Lucas, Robert William, "Performance Coaching: Now and for the Future," *HR Focus,* v71n1, January 1994.

Management and, Coordination Agency, Measures for Pushing Forward Administrative Reform, Tokyo, Japan, 1994.

Markowich, M. Michael, "15 HR Practices That Cost You," *HR Magazine,* May 1993, 105-107.

———, "Who's Running HR?Attorneys?," *Personnel Journal,* v73n5, May 1994.

Martin, John, "Reengineering Government," *Governing,* 1993.

Martineau, Jennifer W and Walter W. Tornow, "Confidence in Leadership," *Issues and Observations,* v14n3, 1994.

Marts, Terri L., *HR Transformation* "Implementing the Reengineered HR," May 1994.

Mascarenhas, R. C., "Building an Enterprise Culture in the Public Sector in Australia, Britain and New Zealand," *Public Administration Review,* July/August 1993, 326-327.

Matthes, Karen, "Empowerment: Fact or Fiction?," *HR Focus,* v59n3, March 1992, 5-6.

———, "Companies Can Make It Their Business to Care," *HR Focus,* v69n2, February 1992, 4-5.

———, "Strategic Planning: Define Your Mission," *HR Focus,* v70n2, February 1993.

McCarthy, Joseph P., "Riding the Third Wave," *Personnel Journal,* v70n4, April 1991, 34-35.

McElrath-Slade, Rose, "Caution: Re-engineering in Progress," *HR Magazine,* June 1994, 54-57.

McGregor, D., "The Staff Function in Human Relations," *Journal of Social Issues,* Summer 1984, 8.

McMahon, Brian, "PerspectivesWhat Quality Dividend?," *The Total Quality Review,* May/June 1994, 5-6.

McManis Associates, Inc., *A Study of Private Sector/State and Local Government Personnel Operations,* McManis Associates: Washington, D.C., 1985.

———, *A Study of Private Sector/State and Local Government Personnel Operations Executive Summary,* McManis Associates: Washington, D.C., 1985.

Mechling, Jerry, "Reengineering: Part of your Game Plan," *Governing,* v7, February 1994.

Mercer, Michael W., "Turning Your Human Resources Department into a Profit Center," AMACOM American Management Association, New York, NY, 1989.

Messmer, Max, "Strategies to Calm Those Restructuring "Jitters"," *HR Focus,* v70n10, October 1993, 18.

Micolo, Anthony, "HR's New Role as Casting Director," *HR Magazine,* August 1993, 19-21.

Microdata, *A Framework for HRM in the Australian Public Service,* Microdata, 1992.

Ministry of Finance, *The World's Best Public Sector?,* Finland, 1993.

Mishra, Aneil K. and Karen E. Mishra, "The Role of Mutual Trust in Effective Downsizing Strategies," *Human Resource Management,* v33n2, Summer 1994.

Moravec, Milan, "Leaders Must Love Change, Not Loathe It," *HR Focus,* v71n2, February 1994, 13.

Morgan, Iris, "The Technology of Information," *Personnel Management,* v24n8, August 1992.

Morrill, Douglas M., Jr., "Human Resource Planning in the 1990s," *Best's Review,* v91n3, July 1990.

Nakanishi, Greg, "Building Business Through Partnerships," *HR Magazine,* v36n6, June 1991.

National Academy of Public Administration, Center for Information Management, *Reengineering for Results: Keys to Success from Government Experience,* August 1994.

———, *Leading People in Change: Empowerment, Commitment, Accountability,* National Academy of Public Administration, June 1993.

———, *Revitalizing Federal Management: Managers and their Overburdened Systems,* National Academy of Public Administration: Washington, D.C., 1983.

Literature Review Summary

———, *Salary Management: Processes to Support Strategic Objectives*, National Academy of Public Administration, Washington, D.C., June 14, 1994.

National Association of State Personnel Executives, *Applications for the Eugene H. Rooney, Jr. Award Recognizing Innovative State HRM Programs*, Lexington, KY, May 1994.

National Commission on the State and Local Public Service, "Hard Truths/Tough Choices," The Nelson Rockefeller Institute of Government: Albany, New York, 1993, 1.

National Performance Review, *Creating a Government That Works Better and Costs Less*, Government Printing Office: Washington, D.C., September 1993.

———, *Creating a Government That Works Better and Costs Less, ED09:Improve Employee Development Opportunities in Department of Education, Accompanying Report of the National Performance Review*, Government Printing Office: Washington, D.C., September 1993.

———, *Creating a Government That Works Better and Costs Less, Improving Customer Service, Accompanying Report of the National Performance Review*, Government Printing Office: Washington, D.C., 1994.

———, *Creating a Government That Works Better & Costs Less, Office of Personnel Management (OPM), Accompanying Report of the National Performance Review*, Government Printing Office: Washington, D.C., September 1993.

———, *Creating a Government That Works Better and Costs Less, Reinventing Human Resource Management, Accompanying Report of the National Performance Review*, Government Printing Office: Washington, D.C., September 1993.

———, *Creating a Government That Works Better and Costs Less, Strengthening the Partnership in Intergovernmental Service Delivery, Accompanying Report of the National Performance Review*, Government Printing Office: Washington, D.C., 1994.

Niven, Daniel, "When Times Get Tough, What Happens to TQM?," *Harvard Business Review* v71, May June 1993.

Nunes, Frederick E., "Experience in Helping Managers: 1968-93," *The Public Manager, The Bureaucrat*, Inc.: Arlington, VA, Spring 1994.

O'Connell, Sandra E., "Doing More With Less," *HR Magazine*, January 1993, 31-33.

———, "Doing More with Less, Part 2," *HR Magazine*, v38n2, February 1993, 33-38.

———, "The HR Automation Budget," *HR Magazine*, v37n7, July 1992, 31-32.

———, "System Redesign Makes FedEx a Technology Leader," *HR Magazine*, v39n4, April 1994, 33-37.

O'Neil, Sandra, "Aligning Pay With Business Strategy," *HR Magazine*, August 1993, 7679.

OECD, "Check Trends in Public Sector Pay: A Study of Nine OECD Countries," *Public Management*, Paris, France, 1994.

Olian, Judy D. and Sara L. Rynes, "Making TQ Work: Aligning Organization Processes, Performance Measures & Stakeholders," *Human Resource Management*, v30n3, Fall 1991.

Orvis, Bruce R. and James R. Hosek, *Pacer Share Productivity and Personnel Management Demonstration: 3rd Year Evaluation*, Rand Corporation: Santa Monica, California, 1993.

Osborne, David and Ted Gaebler, *Reinventing Government – How the Entrepreneurial Spirit is Transforming the Public Sector*, AddisonWesley Publishing Co, 1992.

Overman, Stephanie, "A Day in the Life of An HR Generalist," *HR Magazine*, v38n3, March 1993, 78-79, 82-83.

———, "Big Bang Change: Reengineering HR," *HR Magazine*, v39n6, June 1994, 50-53.

———, "In Search of Best Practices," *HR Magazine*, December 1993, 48-50.

———, "Managing in the Leaner Organization," *HR Magazine*, November 92, 39-43.

———, "Reaching for the 21st Century," *HR Magazine*, v37n4, April 1992.

———, "Nofrills HR at Nucor," *HR Magazine*, July 1994, 5660.

Oxford Associates Aetna Slides, Oxford Associates, 1993, 14.

Oxford Associates, *Best Practices in Business Process Reengineering: A Survey of Fortune 500 Companies*, Oxford Associates, July 1993.

Paduch Peelen, Jean, "Fire When Ready," *The Public Manager, The Bureaucrat*, Inc.: Arlington, VA, Spring 1994.

Palvia, Prashant and Sherry Sullivan, "PRISM Profile: An Employee-oriented System," *HR Focus*, v70n5, June 1993, 19.

Pamplin, Claire, "The New Renaissance Manager," *Executive Directions*, April 1994.

Paranilam, Margaret A., "Increasing Professionalism Required of HR Executives," *Journal of Compensation & Benefits,* January/February 1990.

Pasqualetto, Joe, "HRIS Has Evolved from Capturing Information to Managing Change," *Personnel Journal,* January 1993.

———, "New Competencies Define the HRIS Manager's Future Role," *Personnel Journal,* v72n1, January 1993, 91-99.

Perry, James L., "Transforming Federal Civil Service," *The Public Manager,* v22n3, Fall 1993.

Personnel Management, "Not Ready Yet for Strategic Role?," *Personnel Management,* December 1992, 13.

Peters, Tom, "Damn Bureaucrats," *The Washingtonian,* November 1989, 89-95.

Phillips, Jack J., "13 Ways to Show You're Worth It: A Guide to HR Evaluation," *Human Resources Professional,* v4n2, Winter 1992.

Phillips, Jack J. and Anson Seers, "Twelve Ways to Evaluate HR Management," *Personnel Administrator,* v34n4, April 1989.

Pickard, Jane, "At the Heart of the Business," *Personnel Management,* March 1994.

Plevel, Martin J. and Fred Lane, "AT&T Global Business Communications Systems: Linking HR with Business Strategy," *Organizational Dynamics,* v22n3, Winter 1994, 59-71.

Plug, Bryan, "Don't Ignore Employees," *Computing Canada,* v20n7, March 30, 1994.

Porter, Benson L. and Warrington S Parker, Jr., "Culture Change," *Human Resource Management,* Spring/Summer 1992, 45-67.

Prahalad, C.K and Gary Hamel, "The Core Competence of the Corporation, Gaining Strategic Advantage, *Harvard Business Review,* 3-15.

President's Association, *HR Strategies for the 90's: A Basis for Competitive Advantage,* President's Association: New York, NY, 1990.

President's Council on Management Improvement, *Improving the Management of Human Resources in the Federal Government Through a Private-Public Partnership,* vI, PCMI: Washington, D.C. 1987.

Price Waterhouse, *Shedding Light on Good Ideas: Bright Ideas from Price Waterhouse.*

The Prime Minister, The Chancellor of the Exchequer and the Chancellor of the Duchy of Lancaster, "The Civil Service-Continuity and Change," *A White Paper Presented to the Parliament,* July 1994, 1-4.

Pritchett, Price, *The Employee Handbook for Organizational Change,* Pritchett and Associates, Inc.: Dallas, Texas.

Public Service Commission, *Human Resource Management Framework,* Public Service Commission.

Public Service Commission, "Managing Our People, Human Resources Management Framework," *Australian Public Service Commission Booklet,* 1993.

Reengineering: The HR Perspective, AMA's HR Conference Report, June 1994, 3-6.

Rainey, Hal G., "Rethinking Public *Personnel Management,*" in Ingraham, Pat and Barbara S. Romzek & Associates, *New Paradigms for Government,* 1994, Jossey-Bass: San Francisco, 115.

Ramos, John, "Producing Change that Lasts," *Across the Board,* March 1994, 29-33.

Reynolds, Larry, "Can Government Be Reinvented? Reengineering; Total Quality Management; Yes, Corporate America is Undergoing Radical Change," *Management-Review,* 1994.

Richards-Carpenter, Colin, "How a CPIS Helps Re-engineering," *Personnel Management,* v25n11, November 1993.

Roberts, Deborah, "Reinventing Government, Virginia Style," *UVA Newsletter,* v70, January 1994.

Rosik, Peter, "Building a Customer-Oriented HR Department," *HR Magazine,* v36n10, October 1991, 64-66.

Roth, William F., "Perspectives – Quality, an Opportunity for Human Resources," *The Total Quality Review,* May/June 1994, 7-10.

Runnion, Timm, "Outsourcing Can be a Productivity Solution for the '90s," *HR Focus,* v70n11, November 1993.

Rybka, John S., "Outsourcing Employee Benefits: How to Tell if It's Right for Your Organization," *Employee Benefits Journal,* v18n4, December 1993.

Saha, Sudhir Kumar, "Managing Human Resources: China vs. the West," *Canadian Journal of Administrative Sciences,* v10n2, June 1993.

Sampson, Charles, "Professional Roles and Perceptions of the Public Personnel Function," *Public Administration Review,* March/April 1993, 154160.

Literature Review Summary

Santora, Joyce E., "Alamo's Drive for Customer Service," *Personnel Journal*, April 1991, 42-44.

Savoie, Donald J., "Public Service Reforms: Looking to History and Other Countries," *Optimum*, Summer 1992, 9.

Schaffer, Robert H. and Harlow B. Cohen, "Today's Business Problems Require New HR Strategies," *Human Resources Professional*, Summer 1991.

Schay, Brigitte, "Criteria for Effective HRM Programs," Briefing to Institute for International Research, September 24, 1994.

Scheef, Devon, "Deck for Success," *Training & Development*, v47n9, September 1993.

Schenk, K.D. and Robert L. Holzbach, "Getting the Job Done with HuRBIE: A Human Resources EIS," *Interfaces*, v23n3, May/June 1993.

Sendelbach, Neil B., "The Competing Values Framework for Management Training and Development: A Tool for Understanding Complex Issues & Task," *Human Resources Management*, v33n1, Spring 1993.

Serwer, Andrew E., "Lessons from America's Fastest Growing Companies," *Fortune*, August 8, 1994.

Sherwood, Frank P., "Comprehensive Government Reform in New Zealand," *The Public Manager*, Spring 1992, 23.

Shimko, Barbara Whitaker, "All Managers Are HR Managers," *HR Magazine*, January 1990, 67-70.

Shoop, Tom, "From Citizens to Customers," *Government Executive*, v26, May 1994.

———, "Headlong Into Quality," *Government Executive*, 1993.

Sibson, Robert E., *Strategic Planning For Human Resources Management*, AMACOM, New York, NY, 1992.

Sirianni, Carlo A., "Human Resource Management in Italy," *Employee Relations*, v14n5, 1992.

Smith, Anna, "How do You Spot a Good HR Manager?," *Management-Auckland*, v41n2, March 1994.

Smith, Bob, "Business Process Reengineering: More than a Buzzword," *HR Focus*, v71n1, January 1994, 17-18.

Smith, Raymond W., "Managing Change the Bell Atlantic Way," *Executive Directions*, April 1994, 31-35.

———, "Managing by Commitment: The Bell Atlantic Way," *Futures Research Quarterly*, v9, Summer 1993.

Sobkowiak, Roger T., "Reengineering HRIS to Meet Future Challenges," *Human Resources Professional*, v3n2, Winter 1991.

Society for Human Resources Management, Annual Conference Presentation by Richard W. Beatty, St. Lois, Missouri, June 29, 1994.

———, Notes on SHRM's Program on Compensation Trends and Issues, July 26, 1994.

———, *Professional Certification in Human Resource Management*, SHRM.

———, "SHRM-BNA Survey No. 57&58 – Human Resources Activities, Budgets, and Staffs: 1991-92 & Bulletin to Management – BNA Policy & Practices, Bureau of National Affairs, June 1992, May 1993.

———, *HR Value Analysis Study*.

———, *Detailed Human Resources Audit*.

Society for Human Resources Management Foundation, *The Competency Initiative: Standards of Excellence for Human Resource Executives*, SHRM Foundation.

Spirig, John E., "HRIS Topics: CBT – Computer-Based Training – Holds Key Benefits for a Changing User Community," *Employment Relations Today*, v17n4, Winter 1990.

———, "HRIS Topics: Succession Planning Systems Provide Managers With the Data They Need to Make the Right Choices In Leadership Development," *Employment Relations Today*, Autumn 1990, 249-252.

Spoor, Jim, "You Can Quantify Training Dollars and Program Value," *HR Focus*, May 1993, 3.

Standing, Tom and Jerry Martin, "Attitude Surveys: A Catalyst for Cultural Change," *HR Focus*, v68n12, December 1991.

State of Washington, Washington Management Service Conference Materials, Washington State, June 21, 1993.

Steinburg, Craig, "Partnerships with the Line," *Training & Development*, v45n10, October 1991, 29-35.

Storey, John, "HRM in Action: The Truth is Out at Last," *Personnel Management*, v24n4, April 1992.

Streamlining and Simplifying Administrative Systems, Report of the Auditor General of Canada to the House of Commons 1993, Chapter 6, 170.

Stuart, Peggy, "Getting to the Top of HR," *Personnel Journal,* v71n5, May 1992, 82-91.

———, "Labor Unions Become Business Partners," *Personnel Journal,* v72n8, August 1993.

Stump, Robert W., "Change Requires More Than Just Having a Vision," *HR Focus,* v71n1, January 1994.

Sunoo, Brenda Paik, "HR Positions U.S. Long distance for Further Growth," *Personnel Journal,* v73n6, June 1994.

Szpekman, Andrew H., "Quality Service Sets You Apart," *HR Magazine,* September 1992, 73-74.

Tannenbaum, Scott I. and Lisa M. Dupuree-Bruno, "The Relationship Between Organization and Environmental Factors and the Use of Innovative HR Practices," *Group & Organization Management,* v19n2, June 1994.

Thompson, Curt M., "Preparation is Key To Successful Change," *HR Focus,* April 1994, 17-18.

Thomson, Peninah, "Public Sector Management in a Period of Radical Change: 1979-1992," *Public Money and Management,* July/September 1992, 33-41.

Thornburg, Linda, "Accounting for Knowledge," *HR Magazine,* October 1994, 52.

———, "Growing up with PepsiCo," *HR Magazine,* v38n8, August 1993, 52-53.

———, "HR Executives Focus on StrategicPartner Role," *HR Magazine,* v36n7, July 1991, 62-63.

———, "HR Gears Down to Increase Flexibility," *HR Magazine,* v36n12, December 1991, 72-74.

———, "IBM's Agents of Influence," *HR Magazine,* v38n2, February 1993, 80-83.

———, "Yes, Virginia, HR Contributes to the Bottom Line," *HR Magazine,* August 1993, 6263.

———, "The White Knight of HR Effectiveness," *HR Magazine,* v37n11, November 1992, 67-73.

Tinsley, Dillard B., "Future Flash: Computers Facilitate HR Function," *Personnel,* v67n2, February 1990.

Towers, Perrin and Forster, *Priorities for Competitive Advantage,* 1991.

Treasury and Civil Service Committee, *The Role of the Civil Service Interim Report,* v1, The House of Commons: London, U.K., July 21, 1993.

U.S. Civil Service Commission, *Classification Standards for GS-201-Series,* 1966, 31-34.

———, see various classification standards for GS-200 series positions.

U.S. Department of Labor, *High Performance Work Practices and Firm Performance,* Government Printing Office: Washington, D.C., August 1993.

———, DOL 2000: *Making DOL a Better Place to Work,* Government Printing Office: Washington, D.C., 1989.

———, *American Workplace,* Government Printing Office: Washington, D.C., v2n3, May 1994.

U.S. Department of State, *Reinventing Government: Change at State,* Government Printing Office: Washington, D.C., 1993.

U.S. General Accounting Office, *The Changing Workforce: Demographic Issues Facing the Federal Government,* Washington, D.C., March 1992.

———, *Civil Service ReformDevelopment of 1978 CSR Proposals,* March 31, 1988.

———, *Federal Personnel: Special Authorities Under the Demonstration Project at Commerce,* Washington, D.C., July 1992.

———, *Management of VA: Improved Human Resource Planning Needed to Achieve Strategic Goals,* Washington, D.C., March 1993.

———, *Management Practices: U.S. Companies Improve Performance Through Quality Efforts,* Washington, D.C., May 1991.

———, *Office of Personnel Management: Better Performance Information Needed; Report to the Director,* Washington, D.C., February 2, 1990.

———, *Organizational Culture: Techniques Companies Use to Perpetuate or Change Beliefs and Values,* Washington, D.C., February 1992.

———, *Pay Equity: Washington State's Efforts to Address Comparable Worth,* Washington, D.C., July 1992.

———, *Performance Measurement: An Important Tool in Managing for Results,* Washington, D.C., May 1992.

———, *The Public Service: Issues Affecting its Quality, Effectiveness, Integrity, and Stewardship; Report to Designated,* September 13, 1990.

Literature Review Summary

———, *The Public Service: Issues Confronting the Federal Civilian Workforce,* Washington, D.C., January 1992.

———, *Program Performance Measures: Federal Agency Collection and Use of Performance Data,* Washington, D.C., May 1992.

———, *Quality Management: Survey of Federal Organizations: Briefing Report to the Honorable Donald Ritter,* Washington, D.C., 1991.

———, *TQM Implementation in the Navy,* 1993.

U.S. House of Representatives, Committee on the Budget, *Management Reform: A Top Priority for the Federal Executive Branch,* Government Printing Office, Washington, D.C., 1991.

U.S. Merit Systems Protection Board, *Delegation and Decentralization: Personnel Management Simplification Efforts in the Federal Government: A Report to the President and Congress of the United States,* Government Printing Office: Washington, D.C., 1989.

———, *Entering Professional Positions in the Federal Government,* Government Printing Office: Washington, D.C., March 1994.

———, *Federal Personnel Offices: Time for Change?,* Government Printing Office: Washington, D.C., August 1993.

———, *To Meet the Needs of the Nations: Staffing the US Civil Service and the Public Service of Canada,* Government Printing Office: Washington, D.C.

———, *Working for America: An Update,* Government Printing Office: Washington, D.C., July 1994.

U.S. Office of Personnel Management, *Committees and the Director, Office of Personnel Management,* Washington, D.C.

———, *Digest of Exemplary Personnel Practices,* Washington, D.C., 1993.

———, *Federal Human Resource Management: Strategic Planning Workshop – Draft,* Washington, D.C., May 67, 1993.

———, *Federal Personnel Research Programs and Demonstration Projects: Catalysts for Change,* Washington, D.C.

———, *Human Resources Development Group Establishing the Value of Training,* Washington, D.C., March 1994.

———, *Human Resources Development Group Roles & Competencies of the HR Development Professional in the Federal Government,* Washington, D.C., October 1992.

———, *Manage to Budget Programs: Guidelines For Success,* Government Printing Office: Washington, D.C., August 1989.

———, Notes on OPM Buyout and Retirement Update, August 4, 1994.

———, *Partners for Change: June 1-2 Conference Proceedings,* Washington, D.C., September 1994.

———, *Personnel Systems and Oversight Group, Investing in Federal Productivity and Quality,* Office of Personnel Management, Washington, D.C., November 1992.

———, *Personnel and Oversight Group Survey of Federal Employees,* Office of Personnel Management: Washington, D.C., May 1992.

———, *Seminar On Accountability and the Good Government Framework,* Office of Personnel Management, Washington, D.C., September 27, 1994.

Ulrich, Dave, "A New HR Mission: Guiding the Quality Mindset," *HR Magazine,* December 1993, 51-54.

———, "Human Resources as a Competitive Advantage: Changing Roles and Required Competencies," Presentation to the New Jersey Human Resources Planning Society, November 9, 1994.

Ulrich, Dave and Arthur Yeung, "A Shared Mindset," *Personnel Administrator,* March 1989, 38.

Ulrich, Dave and Wayne Brockbank, "Beyond Belief: A Benchmark for Human Resources," *Human Resource Management,* Fall 1989, 311-335.

Ulrich, Dave, Wayne Brockbank and Arthur Yeung, "Human Resources Competencies in the 1990s," University of Michigan School of Business Administration Study, 27.

United Kingdom, *Making the Most of Next Steps: The Management of Ministers' Departments and their Executive Agencies,* London, U.K., May 1991.

Verlander, Edward G., "Executive Education for Managing Complex Organizational Learning," *Human Resource Planning,* v15n2, 1992.

Vogl, A.J., "Noble Survivors," *Across the Board,* June 1994.

Walker, Alfred, Handbook of Human Resource Information Systems, McGraw Hill, Inc.: Washington, D.C., 1993.

Weatherly, Jonathan D., "Dare to Compare for Better Productivity," *HR Magazine,* September 1992, 42-46.

Weinberg, Raymond B., "Certification Study Guide," Society for Human Resources Management, 1994, 7.

Weinstein, Harold P. and Michael S. Leibman, "Corporate Scale Down, What Comes Next?," *HR Magazine,* August 1991, 33-37.

Werner, Thomas J. and Robert F. Lynch, "Challenges of a Change Agent," *Journal for Quality and Participation,* June 1994, 50-53.

West, Jonathan P. and Evan Berman, *Human Resource Strategies in Local Government: A Survey of Progress and Future Direction,* American Review of Public Administration, September 1993, 279-297.

"What Quality Dividend?," *The Total Quality Review,* May/June 1994, 5-6.

White, Alan F., "Organizational Transformation at BP: An Interview with Chairman and CEO Robert Horton," Human Resource Planning, v15n1, 1992.

Wilhelm, Warren R., "Revitalizing the HRM Function in a Mature, Large Corporation," Human Resource Management, v29n2, Summer 1990, 129-144.

Wilkinson, Adrian and Mick Marchington, "Human Resource's Function," TQM Magazine, v5n3, June 1993.

Woodard, Nina E., "HR at the Center of Change Management: A Model and Its Application at a Midwest Financial Institution," Employment Relations Today, v20n2, Summer 1993, 167-174.

Worklife Report, Strategic Partnerships for Competitive Advantage, Worklife Report, v9n3, 1994.

Wray, Grover N. and Frederick W. Julien, "Internal Audit and Human Resources: A Best Practice?," Internal Auditing, v9n1, Summer 1993.

Yang, John Zhuang, "Americanization or Japanization of HRM policies: A Study of Japanese Manufacturing and Service Firms in the US," Advances in International Comparative Management, v7, 1992.

Zimmerman, John H., "The Demand of the Future: "The Complete Executive"," Human Resource Management, v32n2, Summer/Fall 1993.

Zingheim, Patricia K., Schuster, Jay R., "Linking Quality and Pay," *HR Magazine,* December 1992, 55-59.

Zuck, Alfred M., "The Future Role of OPM," *The Bureaucrat,* Spring, 1989, 20-22.

APPENDIX B

Focus Group Results

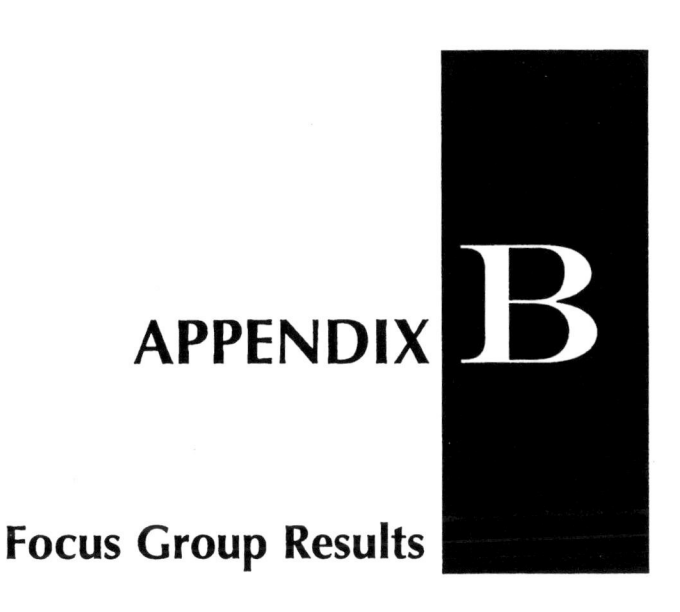

NAPA hosted focus groups in five cities nation-wide to gather data from those people who would be most affected by innovations in human resources practices. There were a total of 69 HR professionals, 50 line managers, and 49 employees who volunteered to participate. The information collected was used to develop models to redefine and restructure agency HRM roles and delivery systems. The five cities included Atlanta, Dallas, New York, San Francisco, and Washington, DC.

The focus group sessions involving HR professionals and line managers in the field differed from those at headquarters for HR professionals and line managers. Unlike traditional focus groups, the Washington, DC sessions were conducted using groupware technology. Groupware is an automated system that allows participants to interact via a network of linked computer stations. Each participant sat at a terminal and typed their answers to the questions. This allowed for everyone to have an equal voice. A NAPA staff member facilitated discussion of each question among the participants. These innovative focus groups generated large amounts of data since everything that was "said" was recorded for later evaluation. The focus groups in the field were traditional focus groups whereby participants vocalized their responses and facilitators recorded the information.

The following analyses combined similar questions into logical groups. The information gathered from all of the focus groups was analyzed and summarized.

FOCUS GROUP TABLE OF CONTENTS

Most Important HRM Issues Facing Organizations	80
Outcome of an Ideal HRM System	82
Ways to Get to an Ideal HRM System	83
HR Skills and Competencies	85
Structure of HR Operations	90
Office of Personnel Management (OPM) Role in the HR of the Future	91
Others' Roles in the HR of the Future	93

Activities to be Discarded 98
Activities to be Contracted or Franchised Out 99
Activities Not Now Being Done but Should Be 100

WHAT ARE THE MOST IMPORTANT HRM ISSUES FACING YOUR ORGANIZATION?

A. HR Professionals

Common Themes

- Everyone and everything is being affected by downsizing
- Changing role of HR office from regulator to advisor
- Gap between National Performance Review (NPR) word and reality
- Field- transition from Health and Human Services (HHS) to Social Security Administration (SSA) independence a big field concern

Major Areas of Disagreement

- Level that HQ should delegate to the field and hold them accountable
- How is hiring being affected
- Whether downsizing or reorganization is the biggest concern

Anecdotal Examples

- There is a "crisis of competence"
- Esprit de corps missing- we need it back

Differences Between Field and DC

- Field is more concerned about employee fears of change
- Field more concerned about labor-management partnerships
- DC more concerned about diversity, automation, and performance (are the right people doing the right work?)

B. Line Managers

Common Themes

- Downsizing a big issue
- Field- coping with change and employees fears very important (morale)
- Field- labor-management: what do partnerships mean?; how to coordinate regional with national unions?
- Ideas are ahead of what can actually be done
- Changing from supervisors to teams

Major Areas of Disagreement
- The field says there is no energy from DC
- Buy-outs are too random – don't deal with organizational priorities

Specific Suggestions/Recommendations
- Need changes in processes in order to do more with less

Anecdotal
- Unions' swing of pendulum- we have to live through it. Only 1 person signed the Executive Order for partnership; unions not set up for them.

Differences Between Field and DC
- DC concerned more about managing to budget (not mentioned in field)
- Leadership issue more important in DC
- Field is more concerned with actually dealing with effects of change, no time to think about automation, diversity, etc.

C. Employees

Common Themes
- Biggest concern is uncertainty about job, whether the agency continue to exist, etc.
- Need process change to deal with increased responsibility
- They are loosing specialists, everyone has to be generalists
- Need training in order to adjust to new roles

Major Areas of Disagreement
- Level of information – some say HQ giving information well while others say only get information from the media
- Some say they want consistency across agencies, contrary to those wanting HR manager flexibility

Specific Suggestions/Recommendations
- Need process change

Anecdotal
- Shouldn't have changed "personnel management" to "human resource management." Neither managers or personnel offices do HRM.

Focus Group Results

WHAT SHOULD BE THE OUTCOMES OF AN IDEAL HR SYSTEM?

A. HR Professionals

Common Themes

- Able to provide timely and accurate information to clients
- More flexibility to do things on-site (hiring, advice, etc.)
- New classification system
- The system needs to be fair and equitable
- Staffing with qualified, productive individuals

Major Areas of Disagreement

- Many think their are too many regulatory obstacles, while some in DC say these are just "smoke and mirrors" and you can get past them

Specific Suggestions/Recommendations

- It isn't enough just to provide many quality people. We need to foster creativity, imagination, risk-taking, and entrepreneurial spirit in the new lean organization.
- If delegate HR responsibilities to managers, train them on how to do it and give them support. Emphasize the importance of accountability, etc. If you don't delegate HR to managers, the personnel office should be supportive, technically knowledgeable, and helpful without regulations causing red tape

Differences Between Field and DC

- In DC they are more concerned about end results as opposed to current problems
- DC has greater focus on mission
- Field concerned about unions as involved, informed partners

B. Line Managers

Common Themes

- Want real, accessible answers at local level
- Need a strategic plan that provides guidance
- Local level needs control and access
- Need a simpler system in terms of classification, hiring, etc
- Need a more efficient system, free from regulations

Major Areas of Disagreement

- The level of centralization that there should be concerning personnel and decision-making policies

Specific Suggestions/ Recommendations
- If a system is good, it's transparent; people don't see the necessity for HR people. We need to train managers to deal with people. The best technicians may not necessarily be the best supervisors

Differences Between Field and DC
- The field does not feel that DC really considers its comments or opinions
- DC more concerned about supervisors getting proper training to make decisions

C. Employees

Common Themes
- Need more and broader training, especially management training
- Want a caring and timely touch by a human
- Give employees more flexibility- combine simpler PD's with work-plans

Major Areas of Disagreement
- The level of guidance needed from OPM or another agency
- The struggle of responsibility between employees and managers
- Who should be there to answer questions – many now will only accept HR answers. They want HR on-site.

Specific Suggestions/Recommendations
- Produce intelligent attractive packages for employees on how to move up to new jobs in 21st century. Offer possibilities and/or training

Anecdotal
- OPM is feared by HR offices.

WHAT DO WE HAVE TO DO TO GET AN IDEAL HR SYSTEM?

A. HR Professionals

Common Themes
- Simplify laws or regulations
- Change the mind-set of HR on all levels, get rid of old roles and focus on the change that is under each person's control
- Commit monetary resources to training
- Be willing to innovate and take risks, then develop what works best

Major Areas of Disagreement
- Should we have a simple decentralized system or organize it at the executive level?

- Should there be stability in federal government employment- i.e. continue the "career bureaucrat mentality" or more competitive employment?
- Should systems (such as personnel data systems) be similar across government agencies, or agency specific?

Specific Suggestions/Recommendations

- We should have control of budget position in field (local level). We can grow/learn from this. We will make mistakes but will improve in leaps and bounds.
- Have HQ establish framework, give flexibility, give performance objectives and get out of the way

Anecdotal

- What do you do if you have no access to anyone "inside the beltway"?

B. Line Managers

Common Themes

- Need top management commitment to change and devotion of time to HR issues
- Need better communication between managers and HR professionals

Specific Suggestions/Recommendations

- Take some action now! Enough talk, enough studies, enough reorganizations of OPM
- Line managers need to see some results from all this activity! Certainly there are areas which few can argue against, start reforming those areas now. Don't wait until all the problems are addressed and resolved—take the first steps now to actually change something which line/field managers can see.
- We need to do our best to get Congress to forgo micro-management and, likewise, get the Office of Management and Budget (OMB) to give up some of their controls like full-time equivalent (FTE) ceilings. Let federal departments and agencies manage under budget controls and be evaluated by bottom-line results. I think this was the message of NPR in their call for movement from "process to results." Unfortunately, although OPM currently seems to be willing to heed this call to a large extent, neither Congress nor OMB have shown much movement. NAPA could do a lot by continuing to chip away at this issue.
- Do benchmarking with private industry to find additional ideas we can try

Anecdotal

- Unless line managers begin to see rapid improvements (rather than talk of what's to come out of NPR), cynicism will increase and managers will not be open to the changes when (if) they come

Differences Between Field and DC

- Not enough field data available to compare differences

C. Employees

Common Themes
- Experiment with pilot projects, encourage risk taking
- Eliminate or relax laws and regulations to allow greater flexibility
- Communicate throughout agency structure
- Cross-train

Specific Suggestions/Recommendations
- Simplify and streamline rules and processes so line managers can do own HRM
- Highlight best practices and share with other agencies

HOW DO HR PROFESSIONALS' SKILLS AND COMPETENCIES NEED TO BE IMPROVED?

A. HR Professionals

Common Themes
- Must expand knowledge base
- Must improve skills: writing, computer, analytic, communicative, organizational, advisory, technical, etc.
- Must have effective problem-solving skills
- Need to improve on timeliness
- Must have sensitivity and understanding for systems approaches
- Process improvements - use innovation and technology
- Must establish certification benchmark

Areas of Disagreement
- The level of automation needed.
- The question of how much power to give to managers.

Anecdotal
- HR professionals come from a lot of different backgrounds and although a lot can be learned from "on the job experience," formal training is imperative for preparation in our future roles.

B. Line Managers

Common Themes
- Need to improve consulting skills
- Must have line management experience
- Need to take a generalist approach
- Must think long range

Focus Group Results

- Must improve skills: analytical, computer, communication
- Training must be ongoing
- Need to be exposed to innovation
- Must treat managers & employees as "customers"
- Flexibility
- HQ must be the leader in team-building
- Must advise managers - do not tell them what to do

Areas of Disagreement

- The common themes illustrate the various improvements that are needed. The participants varied on which skills are most vital - in regards to people skills vs. analytic skills - disagreed on what is more important, but agreed both are necessary.

Anecdotal

- Training is vital to the HQ professional especially since many HQ professionals earned their degrees over 20 years ago — training allows innovation which insures effective service.

C. Employees

Common Themes

- Need to understand the mission of the agency
- Must be familiar with the jobs they staff and service
- Must improve skills: computer skills, communication skills, people skills, analytic skills, business skills, etc.
- Must be able to accommodate change in culture, must be flexible
- Time management - needs to improve
- Must learn to effectively prioritize
- Need cross functional technical training = generalist
- Need to take risks - rely less on rules and regulations
- Must join in on team effort

Major Areas of Disagreement

- All of the employee focus groups agreed that the skills and competencies of HQ professionals must be improved. The common themes represent the general consensus of the ideas suggested.

Specific Suggestions/Recommendations

- Training must be continuous in order to prepare HQ professionals with the skills to serve its customers.

HOW DO LINE MANAGERS' SKILLS AND COMPETENCIES NEED TO BE IMPROVED?

A. HR Professionals

Common Themes

- Need to improve all working skills
- Must be trained to be a competent supervisor
- Training must be ongoing
- Line managers must develop HR skills and perform HR duties
- Need to improve problem-solving techniques
- Must learn to use self-analysis
- Must be accountable for all actions

Anecdotal

- Training is vital to the role of the line manager — a line manager must be orientated with the HRM philosophy in order to put HR functions into action

B. Line Managers

Common Themes

- Need basic management training and skills:
    - learn how to discipline employees
    - learn how to develop employees' skills
    - learn how to deal with employees' problems
- Improve employee evaluation techniques
- Improve writing, computer, business, and analytical skills
- Become an effective communicator — develop people skills
- Must train to develop a clear understanding of HR
- Learn how to form and to be part of a team
- Must learn how to balance budget
- Must learn the most effective methods of performing particular jobs
- Need to develop motivational skills
- Need training in the use of rewards systems
- Need to obtain problem-solving skills

Anecdotal

- Line managers must use HR functions and not rely on HR people do to it for them. HR needs a total team effort in order to be effective.

Focus Group Results

C. Employees

Common Themes

- Need proper training to be a supervisor
- Must build knowledge of HR in order to perform personnel functions
- Must improve skills: computer, writing, analytic, etc.
- Must have people skills and the ability to communicate effectively
- Accountability
- Flexibility - need to be able to respond to change
- Must improve leadership capabilities

Major Areas of Disagreement

- There were no real disagreements but participants had different ways of improving the skills and competencies of line managers. The common themes represent a general consensus.

HOW DO EMPLOYEES' SKILLS AND COMPETENCIES NEED TO BE IMPROVED?

A. Employees (This was the only group that was asked this question)

Common Themes

- Must improve working skills by: increasing computer literacy, learning how to communicate effectively, etc
- Need to be familiar with HRM and personnel
- Flexibility to change
- Must be proactive in seeking information about personnel policies which affect employees
- Need ethics training
- Need to have teamwork skills and mind-set

Major Areas of Disagreement

- Many stated that HR must seek them out with the services it can provide. Others pointed out that employees are the customers and must provide feedback in order to obtain the proper assistance.

HOW WOULD YOU STRUCTURE A HEADQUARTERS HR OPERATION?

A. HQ Professionals

Common Themes

- HQ must coordinate and evaluate field activity, but not control or comment on every issue.

- Structure must eliminate shadow HR operations — can be achieved by centralizing functional processes. This theme contrasted with the idea of decentralizing which would allow each individual office to be involved in all of its functions.
- HQ must oversee policy
- Automation is key to the future of operations. It is a budget issue - it will cost to keep up with technology. Also, HQ must still serve its customers "face to face" - a balance must be found.
- HQ must obtain a position in organization itself and must be an integral part of management
- The consensus on reporting relationships was that it must occur at all levels, everyone must be involved and knowledgeable in order to fulfill agency's mission.
- HQ HR program must be involved in the long term strategic planning of the agency.
- Structure of HQ must be with a team concept
- HQ structure must be formed by "customer feedback" - HQ works for field

Areas of Disagreement
- The focus groups debated the issue of specialists vs. generalists. No clear consesus.
- A very different idea for HQ structure was to consolidate all HQ's into one department of HR with the function of providing services to the "frontline" -obviously caused disagreement - definite concern for quality of service, power issue, etc.

Anecdotal
- DC is forcing regions to downsize, thus forcing it to centralize whether it is good or bad
- Centralization is feared because it could decrease customer service and relations
- It is imperative to take time in (re)structuring HQ operations — do not want to act irrationally

B. Line Managers

Common Themes
- HQ must have a clear definition of its agency's mission in order to have a proper structure
- HQ must be on-site and available to its customers - illustrates that HQ sees the role of its customers and their mission
- Must have an understanding of the positions HQ services
- Centralize processes to HQ - allow for variations due to different sizes of agencies
- HQ must be an advisor and consultant to its customers
- HQ should be structured based upon "customer feedback"
- Team structure must be developed

Focus Group Results

Areas of Disagreements

- The concept of centralizing processes also sparked debate on decentralizing processes. Many thought that decentralizing is more effective because processes would be occurring on-site. There was no consensus on what would be more efficient but the pros and cons of both were discussed. Centralizing – cost effective, allows managers to take on more HR functions, time efficient, etc. Decentralizing – on-site, each office has control of its processes, etc. but it may counteract HQ directions and priorities

- All of the focus groups discussed reporting relationships in which different positions reported to another. The general consensus was that reporting must take place in order to inform all levels. The most common suggestion was for reporting to start from the customers to HR field head, to HQ head, to agency head. However, many took the stance that automation would allow reporting to take place automatically, eliminating the need for a reporting structure.

- The generalist approach conflicted with the specialist approach. Specialists must be utilized in their areas of expertise, but generalists must make up the structure of HQ in order to provide customers with a broad knowledge base. The general consensus was to use both.

Specific Suggestions/Recommendations

- HQ must create a structure that will be flexible to the needs of its customers.

HOW WOULD YOU STRUCTURE A FIELD OPERATION?

A. HQ Professionals

Common Themes

- Field autonomy - field and HQ must stop "we" vs. "they", must support the mission, need the power to manage programs effectively.
- Field HR must have a strong on-site presence – must provide assistance with real interaction
- Base the field structure on "customer feedback"
- Use automation to bridge the gaps of distance (i.e. keep in close contact with HQ - use automation to obtain information needed in field)
- Field HR must be a liaison with HQ
- Field HR must be "local shop"

Areas of Disagreement

- The issue of HQ presence on-site was a topic of debate. Many thought that automation would allow for effective HQ service to customers, however the general consensus was that "face to face" is key to successful customer service.
- The was no consensus on centralizing vs. decentralizing. Many thought it would allow the field the time to effectively serve customers, others felt decentralizing would allow for greater control and involvement.

Specific Suggestions/Recommendations
- Structures must be open to changes in culture.

B. Line Managers

Common Themes
- Must have a field structure in which managers are trusted, give managers autonomy to put policies of HQ into action.
- Structure must have a positive relationship between field & HQ.
- Structure must have all levels informed: customer reports to field, HR field must report to HQ and HQ must report to CEO (head of agency).
- HR field structure must provide the services its customers need - need resources in field

Areas of Disagreement
- Debate between centralized vs. decentralized processes. Many were in favor of centralized because field could then concentrate on directly assisting its customers. But, many wanted decentralized in order to allow direct HR participation in processes.

C. Employees

(Employees were not asked structure questions directly but many comments were made).

Comments from Atlanta employees on structure:
- HR professionals are part of team. HR professionals must be a resource of advice and act as a consultant.
- HR staff must also work with team and report to HQ

This focus group also discussed the issue of centralization versus contracting processing out. Overall, the group decided HQ and the field need to have an on-site presence of some kind.

WHAT IS OPM'S ROLE IN THE HR OF THE FUTURE?

A. Line Managers

Common Themes
- Central support function/guidelines/policy development
- Resource to agencies
- No role for OPM
- OPM's role should be minimal — delegate to agencies
- Complementary roles with HR offices

Focus Group Results

Major Areas of Disagreement

- None

Anecdotal

- The real question should be "Do we need an OPM, and if so, what will it do?"

Differences Between Field and Headquarters

- Headquarters - mentioned challenges presented by political appointees.
- Other comments were similar in nature.

B. *HR Professionals*

Common Themes

- Central agency/governmentwide programs/managing data systems/cross-cutting issues
- Technical assistance/guidance/advice/consultant/facilitator
- Clearinghouse
- Oversight

Major Areas of Disagreement

- Training
    - Provide good-quality training for managers.
    - OPM offers training, but other vendors may be cheaper, better.
    - There are so many contractors for training these days, that OPM's role in training is becoming greatly diminished.
- Recruitment
    - Do away with regulations such as veterans' preference and the "rule of three"
    - OPM does a lousy job of recruiting. They cost too much. Why not let managers do their own recruiting?
    - The recruitment system is lousy, but with a little work it could be improved. Possibly make it a single consolidated source of vacancy information, especially for external applicants. Within one agency we send applicants to 17 different offices to find vacancy announcements. Multiply that across the government and there is a need for an effective one-stop shopping system.

Anecdotal

- Advisor, not traffic cop
- Excepted agencies are a good model for other agencies. They already use OPM as an advisor/consultant because expected agencies have their own systems.
- Would rather see OPM become more of an advisor and ally, rather than imposing the "big brother" mentality of the past.

Differences Between Field and Headquarters
- Headquarters - "Keepers of the Merit Principles"
- Headquarters - Viewed OPM as a Clearinghouse

WHAT IS THE EMPLOYEE'S ROLE IN THE HR OF THE FUTURE?

A. *Employees*

Common Themes
- Responsibility for taking control of own career
- Information/computer technology/processing
- Accountability/responsibility
- Leader/teamwork
- Qualifications—broader skills/better qualified

Major Areas of Disagreement
- One group rejected the notion of employees assuming responsibility for their own development — prevailing view was that they have no ability to make it happen — no decision authority and no resources

Anecdotal
- If you have to ask permission, you are not empowered

Differences Between Field and Headquarters
- No differences

B. *Line Managers*

Common Themes
- Responsibility for own career development
- Increased responsibilities
- Teamwork

Major Areas of Disagreement
- None

Differences Between Field and Headquarters
- None — little input from Field

C. *HR Professionals*

Common Themes
- Automation/computer literacy/processing

- Knowledgeable/active/responsible/accountable
- Responsible for own career development

Major Areas of Disagreement
- None

Anecdotal
- Important Issue: the dichotomy between doing away with the supervisor title and getting those same people to be leaders in the new culture of empowered employees.
- Difficult to deal with many of these issues when you don't have all the cards you need to play. Too much political talk about what's happening and what should happen and no execution of necessary change.
- Constant self development is the rule of the day.

Differences Between Field and Headquarters
- Headquarters — Viewed employees as team members. Field did not discuss teams.

WHAT IS THE LINE MANAGER'S ROLE IN THE HR OF THE FUTURE?

A. Employees

Common Themes
- Accountability
- Mentor/coach/leader/advisor
- Recruitment
- Communicator/liaison between personnel and employees
- Supportive of employees/employee development

Major Areas of Disagreement
- None

Anecdotal
- Change from "do this" to "how can I help you do what you need" mind-set

Differences Between Field and Headquarters
- Field - privatize, move toward the way things are done in the private sector
- Headquarters - placed more emphasis on computer literacy

B. Line Managers

Common Themes
- Leader/facilitator/motivator
- Informed/information provider/communicator
- Accountable/responsible/HR decision-maker
- Reduction of agency rules and regulations

Major Areas of Disagreement
- None

Anecdotal
- Field - some line managers will fail when HR staffs don't have specific rules and answers to provide direction for the managers
- Line managers should have "new" guidelines to communicate the new streamlined HR rules. There was a belief that the "old" Federal Personnel Manual (FPM) guidance is still being used, because change has not been communicated

Differences Between Field and Headquarters
- Headquarters - more focus on teamwork/training/staffing/etc.
- Field - emphasized manager involvement in recruitment

C. HR Professionals

Common Themes
- Leader/counselor/motivator/coach/advisor
- HR decision-maker/responsible and accountable for the personnel activity
- Seek HR advice/call on HR for technical assistance
- Informed information providers

Major Areas of Disagreement
- Headquarters - some concerned with support of HR and employees, others see HR as a "bother"

Anecdotal
- Let's not waste time training managers how to use a broken system. Let's fix the HR system first - then hand it over to managers.

Differences Between Field and Headquarters
- HR professionals in the field were quite concerned with automating their tasks. Employees and HR professionals in the field did not reflect the same concerns. The groups at headquarters were more interested in improved automation.

WHAT IS THE HR PROFESSIONAL'S ROLE IN THE HR OF THE FUTURE?

A. Employees

Common Themes

- Consultant/advisor
- Recruiter
- Generalist
- Customer service
- Advisor for union partnerships/conflict resolution advice/advice of rights
- Mediator/facilitator
- Better system to deal with employee problems resulting from downsizing, restructuring

Major Areas of Disagreement

- None

Anecdotal

- None

Differences Between Field and Headquarters

- Field - viewed HR professional's role as a visionary.
- Field - thought HR professionals should conduct research in HR issues.
- Headquarters - stressed computer literacy.

B. Line Managers

Common Themes

- Consultant/advisors/facilitators
- Provide assistance — not control/consultant to manager
- Responsible/accountable for personnel decisions

Major Areas of Disagreement

- Specialist/generalist
    - Most agreed that HR professionals need to be more flexible and able to support more organizations, and they cannot afford to be so specialized in one area or one organization that they are limited.
    - However, others argued that HR professionals are often generalists who do not have adequate training in specific areas of personnel placement within agencies.

Anecdotal
- First: Get the right people in leadership positions
- Second: Train those leaders well to make critical personnel decisions and have them work closely with HR advisors.
- Third: Empower those managers to make critical personnel decisions and support those decisions.

Differences Between Field and Headquarters
- Headquarters was more concerned with employee development.

C. HR Professionals

Common Themes
- Career counselor/advisor/consultant
- Consistency in automation
- Develop/implement/interpret HR policies from OPM broad guidelines
- Customer service
- Strategic partner/planner

Major Areas of Disagreement
- Specialist/generalist
    - The HR role depends on the culture of the agency. There is a need for less specialization and more generalization so we can offer better service to our managers.
    - A good expert/specialist can also be a generalist, can see the whole picture.
    - As long as we are governed by too many regulations, standards, laws, decision managers will need to call on experts, not generalists.
    - We need to be looking at simplifying the process and reducing the number of regulations and laws.
    - Must be able to move across the board, so generalist must have experts to consult with.
    - Near term, generalists may not be trained to be advisor/consultant.

Anecdotal
- There are perhaps three mutually exclusive roles:
    - Advisor/consultant
    - Gatekeeper/police
    - Maintenance/support

Differences Between Field and Headquarters
- Field - Should be able to make decisions at local level, not have to go to headquarters.

WHAT HR PRACTICES/ACTIVITIES CAN BE DISCARDED?

A. HR Professionals

Common Themes

- Paper intensive systems (hard copies of Official Personnel Folder [OPF], File retention rules)
- Performance appraisals

Many others were listed, but the respondents (in every population) commented on ways to alter or streamline the current practices, not to totally discard them.

What HR Practices/Activities Should be Changed?

- Classification system: position audits and the Civilian Personnel Office (CPO) process
- Hiring process

Major Areas of Disagreement

- There was no disagreement

Anecdotal Examples

- Few functions can really be discarded; they need to be altered or streamlined
- We should look at the functions being done that do not add value and get rid of them. Example: We need to identify the unnecessary reports.

Differences between Field and DC

This is not applicable because the individual answers varied regardless of geographical location; they were all very different answers.

B. Line Managers

Common Themes

- Paper intensive practices

Major Areas of Disagreement

- There was no disagreement

Anecdotal Examples

- Throw out the OPM system and start over with a new one that meets manager's needs

Differences Between Field and DC

N/A

C. Employees

Common Themes
- Performance appraisal system

Major Areas of Disagreement Between the Field and DC
- None

Anecdotal
- None

Specific Suggestions/Recommendations
A Dallas employee said that in the complaint process, the third-line supervisory complaint resolution step should be eliminated. It should stop at the second line effort to resolve/decide the complaint.

WHAT HR PRACTICES/ACTIVITIES SHOULD BE CONTRACTED OR FRANCHISED OUT?

A. HR Professionals

Common Themes
- Training
- Employee Assistance Programs (EAPs)
- Payroll

Major Areas of Disagreement
- None

Anecdotal Examples
Some HR professionals said that all HR practices can be franchised out, but that cost analysis and effectiveness studies should be done to see that it would work better than current in-house functions. Some managers like to "reach out and touch" — therefore would want to franchise out.

Differences Between the Field and DC
A DC HR professional suggested closing the regional HR centers.

B. Line Managers

Common Themes
- Training
- Dispute resolution activities
- Benefits management

Focus Group Results

Major Areas of Disagreement

- None

Anecdotal Examples

- A line manager in Washington said that historically, contracting out costs more. And, almost everything can be contracted out.
- A DC line manager said there should be an expert [computer] system that would have expertise concentrated in a few places so that HR generalists can tap into the information as needed.
- Another DC line manager suggested a 900 number for the tough questions. An expert would be hired to answer those questions.

Differences Between the Field and DC

N/A

C. Employees

Common Themes

- All
- Training

Major Areas of Disagreement

- None

Specific Suggestions/Recommendations

- In San Francisco the employees were clearly against franchising out employee relations because it is too sensitive and the history and knowledge is needed.
- An employee from New York said that the criteria for franchising should be cost, better process or methodology [than the agency can accomplish], and responsiveness of the contractor.
- Several employees in Dallas had comments about franchising: Anything can be franchised, but this is not a good idea due to loss of ownership; the loss of accountability could be a result of contracting out; and oversight of the contractor would still require in-house skills.

Differences Between Field and DC

N/A

WHAT HR PRACTICIES/ACTIVITIES ARE NOT NOW BEING DONE BUT SHOULD BE?

A. HR Professionals

Common Themes

- Some type of strategic or long-range planning.

- Automation/technological innovations
- Career counseling

Major Areas of Disagreement
- None

Specific Suggestions/Recommendations
- One HR professional in DC said that employees want financial counselors but the reality gap is that this is too difficult.

Anecdotal
- None

B. Line Managers

Common Themes
- No clear consensus

Major Areas of Disagreement
- None

Anecdotal Examples
In DC, a line manager said that HR should manage individuals to take responsibility for their careers and development plans.

Differences Between the Field and DC
- None

C. Employees

Common Themes
- No Clear Consensus

Major Areas of Disagreement
There was disagreement between an employee and a line manager regarding development. In this category, the line manager said the employee should take charge of his/her own career and development plans. An employee from Dallas remarked that supervisors should be accountable for maintaining employees' skills and performance.

Anecdotal Examples
- An employee in DC commented that HR should perform research and benchmarking, then share the information.
- In Atlanta, employees said that agencies want their own personnel staff who work for their agency's goals to do their functions, not people who work for another agency's goals.

Focus Group Results

Differences Between the Field and DC

N/A

Clearly there was little consensus among the populations in the different cities for the last three questions. The answers were as varied as the number of people at the sessions. The last question was most difficult to summarize because the responses were so varied. For instance, many people mentioned training; however, an employee recommended basic training on HR systems, an HR professional recommended motivation training, and line managers said creative problem solving and diversity training. According to the responses, every HR function can be contracted or franchised out. Only one person mentioned something that should not be contracted out: an employee from San Francisco said that employee relations should not be contracted out because it is too sensitive, and the history and knowledge is needed to work through the problem. However, many respondents mentioned that various parts of the complaint resolution process should be contracted out. Many of the suggestions were used in various places elsewhere in this report.

APPENDIX C

A Report on Human Resources Management Factors Unique to Small Federal Agencies

Internal Staff Report to the Study Group on:

Implementing Real Change in Human Resources Management

October 1994

CONTENTS

INTRODUCTION	104
OBJECTIVES	104
METHODOLOGY	104
FINDINGS	105
CONCLUSIONS	108
OBSERVATIONS	109
ITEMS TO CONSIDER DURING THE COURSE OF THE STUDY	110
AGENCY CONTACTS	112

A Report on Human Resources Management Factors Unique to Small Federal Agencies

I. INTRODUCTION

The National Academy of Public Administration (NAPA) is currently engaged in a multi-part study, Implementing Real Change in Human Resources Management: Alternatives for Federal Agencies, sponsored by 32 federal agencies. A significant number of these agencies are considered to be in the category of "small agencies." At meetings with the project staff members, agency representatives have stated that small agencies are "different", and that the differences must be recognized during the study. A decision was made to gather information relating to this issue. The study group initially made a number of working assumptions from which to proceed. As examples:

- Because of their size, small agencies have to operate in a manner and under conditions unlike the larger organizations.
- In addition, there are certain HRM-related factors and issues which are unique to small agencies, and should be taken into account during the course of the study.
- Further, study conclusions and recommendations, in particular, must have a "fit" to the organizations to which they are applied.

With these basic premises in mind, NAPA proceeded to research the relevant factors and issues to isolate and identify them prior to the major study efforts, in order for the study to be truly comprehensive.

II. OBJECTIVES

1. To identify those HRM-related issues and factors which affect only small federal agencies, chiefly as reflected in the views of these agencies.
2. To compare those issues and factors with related areas in larger agencies, in order to analyze, identify, and measure the differences in operations between the two, and any identifiable differences in impact (i.e., effectiveness and efficiency).
3. To gauge the impact of the identified issues on small agency HRM operating capacity.
4. To produce an internal staff document to serve as a basis or template for the main study in considering small agency operations.

III. METHODOLOGY

This effort was planned as a short duration study, with a scheduled completion date of October 31, 1994. Because of the short time span, efforts were made to limit the number of contacts, yet provide sufficient sampling to produce a valid body of information. A combination of telephone interviews, questionnaires, and one formal group meeting was used to sample the small agencies, chiefly using the Human Resources staffs within the agencies. A limited literature search of library databases was conducted. Contact was made with the chairs of the Small Agency Council, the Interagency Advisory Group, and the Small and Independent Agency Personnel Directors Group, as well as with the Office of Personnel Management. In total, 15 agencies were surveyed by at least one of the above methods. (See list of agencies contacted on page 11). Only two of the agencies returned questionnaires as of the report completion date; probably due to the short response time requested. It is possible that more will be returned, and any such replies should be considered during the course of the project.

The literature search was unfruitful. Some few titles dealt with small organizations or businesses, but were confined to issues wholly unrelated to human resources management.

IV. FINDINGS

Although agencies characterized as small may share a number of characteristics, it became evident that no two are completely alike. Some number under 200 employees, while others approach 6,000. Entire organizations are based in the Washington, D.C. area alone, while others have field components also. A number have a single mission and one major occupational group; others are more diverse. Within the context of human resources management, their similarities, which are in fact the main "differences" when compared to larger organizations, are based on the effects of relative size on HRM operations. For that reason, "small agencies" can be looked upon as a catch-all category, based not on function but on the necessity of often ignored small organizations to have a unified voice in governmentwide operations, (as represented by the Small Agency Council), and the sharing of common interests, problems, and occasionally pooled resources. No formal equivalent group exists within the Interagency Advisory Group for large or medium-size organizations; an indication that the imperative to band together is probably more situational, and is likely to be manifested more at those times when interests coincide than as a constant entity.

The following is a list of the differences, as reported by the small agencies contacted:
1. Fewer HR resources (staff and funding) are available.
2. There is less specialization within the HR operations staffs.
3. No separate "Policy" staff; operations and policy are usually performed by the same people.
4. Line managers are responsible for more of program implementation, than is the case with larger organizations.
5. Less money. Funding is often unavailable or inadequate for support, such as equipment, automation initiatives, and training.
6. Fewer "constituencies" to deal with, fewer bureaucratic levels, less red tape.
7. Timeframes for implementation are usually shorter ("things happen fast").
8. Written policy is relied upon less, or when used it is more general and less complex than in other, larger, organizations.
9. Communications are better and faster due to fewer organizational layers, more centralized structures, smaller size in general, fewer parallel organizational components, etc.
10. OPM is generally relied upon more for guidance, although some agencies report that this practice may be diminishing.

11. Consortiums are occasionally formed among several agencies to pool resources for a common end, e.g., SES Certification, training.

12. "Mindset" This refers to the ignoring of small agency views, suggestions and "differences" by larger agencies, OPM, top departmental levels, etc. This phenomenon can be looked upon as more of an effect and a problem area than a difference.

13. Change is not difficult in small agencies, particularly when it involves a governmentwide issue.

When asked whether these perceived differences really impacted upon HR operations (i.e., positively, negatively, or not at all), the agencies' replies indicated that while some factors such as resources and money, could cause problems, others produced real advantages. For example, fewer organizational levels, and (sometimes) completely centralized operations are, in the main, seen to have positive impacts upon communications, speed of implementations, and streamlining of regulations and policy. Conversely, these same advantages, coupled with the cultural push of small agencies to get things done quickly, seemed to produce a strain on limited HR resources when these resources were employed beyond everyday operations.

The greater number of differences cited by the small agencies relate directly to size, in terms of total agency strength, and to the resources allocated to HRM activities. Others appear to be a function of agency structure and/or mission, such as the expectation that events move quickly, for instance, in implementing a new initiative or program. Even in these situations, size has an indirect bearing. It is unlikely that this cultural expectation for a sustained rapid pace of action could long exist in a large organization, regardless of mission or structure. Small agencies can move faster because, as a rule, they are unencumbered by the multiple bureaucratic layers, the large field components, and the multiple constituencies prevalent in large organizations.

Because most differences are attributable to size, we must recognize that we are speaking in relative terms. Large organizations are also different, when compared to medium-sized or small agencies. The key point is in how operations may be affected by differences. What became apparent in analyzing these differences is that there is no ideal size or configuration, and that there are a number of trade-offs involved at every level of size. Differences can be either advantageous to organizations, or can generate liabilities. There is no clear-cut "best situation."

The participating organizations, speaking in terms of their HR organizations, considered the following to be the major disadvantages resulting from the differences cited:

1. Human Resources organizations do not have the staff depth, either in terms of numbers or staff expertise, to comprehensively deal with both day-to-day operations and policy initiatives. They are not generally equipped to develop or design policy and programs, and implement these, without seriously impairing everyday operations.

2. Funding is often limited for support mechanisms, such as equipment, automation, and training, each of which could help to lessen the demands on staff resources.

3. Because top management expects quick action, HR is not given long time-frames for implementation of new initiatives, once decisions have been reached to do so.

4. Not as self-sufficient, comparatively, as larger organizations, and cost per unit of work may be higher. Small agencies heavily depend on a number of external HR and other sources (e.g., payroll systems) to meet policy development goals. These sources include OPM, contractors, consortia of small agencies, "piggybacking" on the work of larger organizations, etc.

5. New initiatives from OPM, congress, other agencies, etc. rarely take cognizance of the impact on small agency resources. Examples cited were the NPR/OPM action on the FPM, reports requirements from agencies such as EEOC and GSA, and legislation for downsizing HR without classification guidelines.

Conversely, the scale of small agency operations is said to produce the following advantages in HR operations:

1. Less time is required to effect changes, implementations, etc., due chiefly to less layering, fewer individual constituencies, more controlled environments, and better communications.

2. Operating managers are more involved in implementation of HR policy, as compared to managers in larger agencies. This is both a difference, as noted previously, and a desirable situation, i.e., a good practice according to generally accepted management principles.

3. More flexibility. Less reliance on written policy; less "red tape." Can sometimes use regulations almost verbatim.

4. Adaptability. The Small Agency Council provides a vehicle to pool resources, to network, and to form working groups as needed.

5. Closer working relationships exist between the HR staff and top agency management.

Taken in perspective, the small agencies have adapted to function effectively within their special environments. The same, of course, can be said of the larger organizations. In either case, where the "difference makes a difference" probably lies more within the unique needs of each organizational type, than in the final result. In small agencies these unique needs are mainly a function of size.

According to the agencies surveyed, these needs* include:

- Models resulting from the NAPA study. A number of agencies stated that the models should be tailored for use by the line managers, who would be responsible for implementation. Models should also be simple or basic, with optional add-ons (modules). Small agencies can serve as "test beds," to sell innovations to larger agencies.

---

*Note that a number of these needs are stated in non-generic terms, ostensibly aimed at the NAPA study. More likely, these needs are a reflection of the general concern centering on the lack of policy development staff resources.

- Whenever possible, preliminary findings from the study should be provided (even drafts). The agencies feel that the study time frames may be too long for them; some not being aware that some deliverables would be completed well before the study termination.
- Tapes of any seminars, symposia, or other proceedings connected to this study should be produced by NAPA, and made available to the small agencies. It may be that here again the sponsoring agencies may not realize that their HR staffs' attendance at these functions is part of the study contract.
- NAPA study needs to address implementation, and "put academics aside."
- Continued recognition of the views and needs of the small agencies by OPM, the larger agencies, and other areas of the federal government. NAPA should provide briefings to the Small Agency Council.
- Communications. A suggestion was made for a small agency (computer) bulletin board, such as OPM used for buyout information. In addition, an information exchange system for small agencies is needed; possibly an interagency e-mail system. A contact list would also be helpful.

Other stated needs were more general, and would likely apply to all government organizations:

- More OPM initiatives such as its clearing house, bulletin boards, and customer orientation on the buyout issue ("Exceptionally helpful")
- More management support for reinvention
- Legislation for broad-banding, streamlining, procurement, non-monetary recognition, etc.
- More independence ("like to design our own systems")

In addition, although never directly addressed as a need, was the issue of resources such as staffing and funding. Expectations for relief in this area appear to be low or non-existent, which may account for the lack of direct discussion of resources as a need during the agency contacts. Another possibility is that the NAPA study is seen as having little potential to affect resource allocations.

V. CONCLUSIONS

The small agencies are essentially correct in their assertion that they are different, in some respects, when compared to others. The differences are, for the most part, directly attributable to relative size, which in turn dictates the resource availability for HR operations. Most, if not all, of the issues and factors unique to small agencies human resources management are generated as a result of this situation. From the research information, one can conclude that, in general, these agencies are able to meet their HRM goals as well as the larger organizations. However the routes taken may significantly differ with respect to how the means to do the job are acquired and used, and stresses on the small agency HR system may be somewhat greater. There is usually no umbrella of a larger parent organization, no separate policy staff, and "economy of scale" leaves very little breathing room or cushion, if any, to depend upon. Still, most agreed that small agencies are in good shape, with the possible exception of training for HRM. A paramount concern, it seems, is for recognition of small agency views, capacities, and differences (which translates as a group of special needs) whenever new HRM initiatives are contemplated. Although couched in terms of what they are seeking from this study, small agencies require more detailed, easily implemented or adaptable models for HR changes, in general. Because of resource limitations, they are looking for specific "how to" information rather than generalized methodologies, and for virtual "off the shelf" systems. As a number of them stated, they haven't the time to become specialists.

From all the information gathered, it is evident that the small agencies see the differences as impacting chiefly upon the policy development aspects of HRM. The agencies' HR offices consist mostly of generalists doing day-to-day work, with no separate staffs or depths of expertise to accomplish policy/development objectives. Simultaneous work in both areas is nearly impossible. Reinforcing this picture is the fact that most of the cited "unique to small agency" needs relate to anticipated NAPA deliverables, such as models, which would substantially cut down on resources agencies would expect to expend on developing policy or systems. Further, none of the agencies expressed significant anxiety concerning implementation capacity; they obviously believe that they can operate in this area as well as any organization.

VI. OBSERVATIONS

The size-related differences cited by the small agencies are a fact of life. The HRM resources picture is hardly expected to improve in the foreseeable future, and the acquisition of policy/development staffs is improbable at best. The situation may be further exacerbated by downsizing initiatives, coupled with increased emphasis on customer service.

It is probably too early in the project to reasonably predict what form some or all of the deliverables will take. Whether or not we can effectively tailor the study products to small agency needs, as in the case of models, will be answered definitively much further into the project.

One suspects the answer is yes, but this will depend on the synthesis of research and analytical results. While the small agencies feel they are operating under a different time imperative, and require study products earlier than the timelines agreed to, this should not drive the project timetable. It is also not good practice to disseminate drafts to agencies, before they have been approved through the Academy process. Some of the agencies have obviously missed the point that the main project is aimed at implementation, and not interim relief. What then, can the study group do to meet the stated needs or concerns of the small agencies during the course of the project? Based upon the comments of the agencies, the following are suggested:

1. Establish a formal liaison with the Small Agency Council, with the purpose of NAPA staff providing briefings, progress reports, etc. on a fairly regular basis at their meetings, if this is mutually agreeable. Attendance at these meetings might also prove useful in keeping current with small agency activities, problems, and needs.

2. Ensure that project staff remains aware of small agency resource concerns, particularly during the product development stages of the project.

3. Although the concept may be impractical because of small agency resource

concerns, look into the possibility of obtaining a small agency IPA or detailee to the project, since no one presently on the project staff has significant small agency experience. The presence of a small agency person would serve to provide a balancing factor during the course of the study.

4. Convene a group of small agency representatives to discuss and possibly formulate an approach to OPM concerning interagency communications (the small agency bulletin board, e-mail, etc., previously discussed).

5. Although a small agency representative is on the Executive Committee of the IAG, there is an apparent need for further input into policy discussions. NAPA should discuss with the Chair of the IAG the possibility of securing an invitation for a representative of the Small Agency Council to attend meetings of any ad hoc group of the large agencies. If this could be accomplished, the views of the small agencies could at least be heard before any major proposals or initiatives are brought before the main IAG.

In summary, the project team members, by remaining aware of small agency concerns throughout the life of the project can ensure that these concerns will be considered at each step. Whether or not most or all can be successfully met from the small agency viewpoint will depend on a number of factors which may be beyond the control of this group, such as further downsizing impacts, the effects of NPR initiatives, etc. NAPA can take a number of proactive steps also, if these are feasible, such as brokering some of the above needs with OPM and the IAG. In any event, judging from their past performances, the small agencies will make good use of any product coming out of this study.

VII. ITEMS TO CONSIDER DURING THE COURSE OF THE STUDY

MODELS (GENERAL): Small agencies look to NAPA for models. They have requested basic models, with optional modules, or add-ons, to use as the situation requires. As an alternative, can models be designed specifically for small agency use, or is the modular route the most effective?

DOWNSIZING: Small agencies are facing arbitrary reduction goals, in HRM and in general. Because of size constraints, fewer options or downsizing strategies appear to be available to these organizations. Is the project capable of designing and offering fresh alternatives to cope with this situation?

COOPERATION: Should small agencies expand the role of "regionalism" or interagency cooperation with small and large organizations?

1. In areas of the country where few HR resources are located, or even at the national level, should small agencies look for more reimbursable support services from large agencies, (e.g., payroll, labor relations, classification, retirement counseling), than they do at present?

2. Should small agency consortia be employed more often? Should NAPA develop guidelines?

3. Although resources are limited, should the use of contractors, experts, etc. be expanded? Should small agencies pool resources to do so?

OPM'S ROLE: Traditionally OPM has been more depended upon by smaller agencies, with more direct interaction than is seen with larger agencies. With the sunset of the FPM, OPM's downsizing and moving toward a more consultative role, small agencies believe some of the support mechanism is being withdrawn. What should OPM be doing to ease these concerns, and should the NPR be made aware of these concerns through NAPA?

BROADBANDING: If size difference impacts upon classification, will that equate to a difference in the models, or will it call for little or no difference in construction?

HRM STAFFING: Does the study group need to ensure that it addresses the fact that small agency staffs are "thin," and apt to get thinner, i.e., how are they going to perform their day-to-day work, and how will they develop policy and implement change?

PARTNERSHIP: How valid is the concept of partnership councils in the small agencies, especially in those numbering under 100 employees? Are there workable alternatives or modifications?

DISPUTE RESOLUTION: Are there more effective options for small agencies in handling EEO complaints, grievances, arbitrations, etc., such as pooling resources, contracting out or receiving support from larger agencies?

REPORTS: Reports requested by other agencies, such as OPM, GSA, and GAO, by Congress, and others make little differentiation in agency size, and the impacts of these requests on resources. Should NAPA look into encouraging these initiators to seek reports mainly from the larger agencies which have the bulk of the employees, problems, etc., in the government? Statistically, the small agencies, even in the aggregate, have little impact on the figures, and extrapolation could give similar results.

NAPA'S ROLE: Should the Academy, as represented by the project, play a proactive role as "honest broker" between the small agencies and OPM, GSA, the NPR and others in meeting some of the small agency needs? Examples include the small agency computer bulletin board, an interagency e-mail system, and closer liaison with ad hoc large agency groups within the IAG.

PROTOTYPES OR PILOTS: Some of the small agencies advocated their use as "test beds" for NAPA models, as a means to sell the idea to larger agencies (and of course benefit from development themselves). Is the idea feasible, and would it give any advantage in marketing? Consider the small agency complaint that their ideas and situations are often ignored. Would success in a small agency environment necessarily be credible to large organizations?

TAPES: Should seminars and symposia be videotaped and provided to small agencies? There is the possibility that non-sponsoring agencies may never attend any of the proceedings, but might be willing to purchase a tape as a training vehicle. Marketing impact and potential wide coverage need to be balanced.

AGENCY CONTACTS

- DEFENSE CONTRACT AUDIT AGENCY (I)
- DEFENSE INFORMATION SYSTEMS AGENCY (M)
- DEFENSE NUCLEAR AGENCY (M)
- EXPORT-IMPORT BANK (M)
- FEDERAL COMMUNICATIONS COMMISSION (M)
- FEDERAL ELECTIONS COMMISSION (I)
- FEDERAL RETIREMENT THRIFT BOARD (I)
- MERIT SYSTEMS PROTECTION BOARD (M)
- NATIONAL ARCHIVES & RECORDS ADMINISTRATION (Q)
- NATIONAL SCIENCE FOUNDATION (I)
- OFFICE OF PERSONNEL MANAGEMENT (I)
- OVERSEAS PRIVATE INVESTMENT CORPORATION (I)
- PEACE CORPS (Q)
- PENSION BENEFIT GUARANTEE CORPORATION (I)
- SECURITIES & EXCHANGE COMMISSION (M)

(I) INTERVIEW
(M) GROUP MEETING
(Q) QUESTIONNAIRE

APPENDIX D

Clusters of Functions[1]

Sustainable Organizational Health

This cluster of functions relates to the functioning of the workforce, most specifically, its productivity. There are, a wide variety of sub-functions that impact upon this strategic HR functional activity: the definition of a labor-management philosophy and strategy; leadership philosophy and style; the health and safety of employees in the workplace; positive/corrective management practices as these relate to the absence of harassment in the workplace; support for investigation and redress activities; the management of sick leave; the provision of employee assistance programming to combat stress or dysfunctional work behaviors resulting from work, personal, financial or family problems; incentive and recognition programs; and employee health and morale surveys.

Continuous Learning Strategies

This cluster of functions relates to the means by which an organization uses training and development as a strategic instrument to ensure organizational effectiveness. Also included in this element are the strategies by which an organization creates and maintains a continuous improvement and continuous learning culture in order to enhance productivity and to be flexible in meeting emerging or unanticipated challenges or opportunities. This function is instrumental in supporting the ongoing competencies (operational, managerial, technological) of the workforce, in assisting management to create and sustain a positive organizational/leadership culture, in "re-skilling" employees affected by workforce adjustment by assisting in the acquisition of new skills, in addressing literacy challenges to a flexible, continuously learning workforce, and in determining the options for training and providing systems to support those options. In addition, organizational development strategies and support, particularly as these relate to the management of change, management effectiveness, teambuilding, participative management styles and strategies and so on would be included in this HR cluster of functions which support continuous improvement and learning.

---

[1]"Guidelines for Determining HR Functions and Delivery Options" developed as a mutual project by Canada's Human Resources Policy Branch and the Personnel Renewal Council. September 1993.

Clusters of Functions

Organizational Analysis and Design

In the broadest, most strategic sense, this cluster of functions refers to the manner by which the department/agency organizes itself to conduct its business and deliver its mandate. Various elements impact upon these decisions including organizations size, geographic distribution of clients of the parent organization, the nature of the business (does service depend upon face-to-face client contact or can it be provided through technological support?), the responsiveness and cost-effectiveness of organizational design options, the general or specialized nature of functions to be performed by the parent organization and so on. This cluster of functions would include the organizational analysis and design functions, but also the more traditional classification and job description development functions. Further, this cluster will need to interface with colleagues in the employment strategies cluster of HR functions to determine the viability of various organizational design options such as contracting out various elements of the department/agency's business versus the need to retain internal departmental or agency resources, or to ensure internal career path development options to ensure organizational effectiveness. In addition, consultation with colleagues in financial services will be required to develop cost-benefit analysis models and options.

Employment Strategies

This cluster of functions is designed to ensure the organization has a competent, productive, sustainable workforce. The sub-functions would include most viable workforce planning and modelling, employment equity and diversity management, workforce adjustment, performance management and staffing. On a strategic basis, this function would support organizational planning to meet projected operational requirements, including the projection and management of attrition, planning of workforce modifications to meet organizational change resulting from streamlining, restraint or austerity measures, the analysis of workforce and labor market demographics, the requirement for new or modified skills to meet future challenges, the "organizational culture" interventions to support the management of a diverse workforce, the identification of strategies to address employment equity requirements, the redeployment and retraining of staff affected by workforce adjustment requirements, the recruitment, deployment and promotion of staff to meet immediate, medium term and long term organizational requirements, the assessment of "most viable workforce" options to maintain organizational integrity (i.e. corporate balance of term/indeterminate, use of part time, job indeterminate members of the workforce) and so on. On a day-to-day operational basis, a staffing specialist would be expected to advise the client manager on options which would also be supportive of the larger organizational objectives in order to assist in ensuring that each staffing action is used as an opportunity to meet organizational objectives in an environment of diminishing opportunity for workforce modification.

Compensation Management

This cluster of functions also subsumes a number of more traditional HR functions: the processes for supporting management input to compensation and benefit bargaining; the equity of compensation between occupational groups and individual positions, as well as equity in what had been traditionally male or female occupation compensation; the administration of compensation and benefits to ensure employees morale and basic counselling services (particularly as these will relate to future choices in benefits packages); retirement planning; separation options and benefits; etc. This area may become increasingly vital if development of job description relativities change to eliminate job descriptions and move to multiskilling or competency-based bargaining compensation methodologies, or if changes to collective bargaining processes occur to permit more department/agency specific negotiations. Further, departments/agencies which require significant levels of overtime or shift work may rely heavily upon this area of activity to contribute to employee satisfaction (or avoid employee dissatisfaction) with routine pay processes.

Management Development and Support

This is a relatively small but critical area of the HR functional support. Organizational effectiveness is directly affected by the quality and sustainability of the leadership cadre in the department/agency. This cluster of functions would include feeder group (particularly high flyer) development and management, executive staffing and development, executive support services including compensation, counselling, mentoring, training, information exchange, lifestyle and work balance strategies, outplacement counselling, etc.

Management of the HR Function

The preceding sections have focused upon the discrete functions and services the HR function provides to its parent organization, either internally or by facilitating the delivery of the service through franchising services or by contracting out the activity. However, in designing the complete HR function, and to ensure its continuing effectiveness, some attention must be given to the management of the function itself. Again, there are a variety of elements that must be considered and options for in-house or external resourcing of the elements must be identified and assessed based upon factors such as the business of the organization, its culture, structure, operating environment, cost effectiveness and affordability.

For each of the above client service functional areas of activity, there must be mechanisms to ensure quality control, monitoring and evaluation, as well as mechanisms to assess and monitor client satisfaction; to enable continuous improvement strategies with a view to streamlining and simplifying services to make them more flexible, responsive and cost-effective; to enhance the use of technology within the function, between functions, between collegial corporate services and between departments and agencies; and to enable the administrative functioning of the HR activity (i.e., printing, travel, equipment maintenance, etc). Mechanisms must be developed to identify and share best practices within and between organizations. In addition, there are responsibilities associated with liaising with central agencies to facilitate a partnership approach to the development of polices and programs which will have governmentwide application. In this area, it is important to note that corporate (governmentwide) objectives for the management of people are respected and implemented. Internal management of expertise, including recruitment, deployment and development are essential to long-term effectiveness.

Although these elements should be transparent to the individual clients in the organization, the structure and resourcing of the HR function by the parent organization must include consideration of these elements if the parent organization is to be well served in the medium to long term.